PHYSICAL EDUCATION and the COMPUTER

by
Mike Skinsley

THE LING PUBLISHING COMPANY LIMITED

3

Dedicated to

Liz, Peter, Helen and Sarah.

Copyright © Mike Skinsley 1987

First published 1987

Published by
The Ling Publishing House
162 King's Cross Road,
London, WC1X 9DH
England.

Skinsley, Mike

1. Physical Education

2. Computers

I. Title

ISBN 0-900 985 18 6

British Library Cataloguing in Publication Data

Typeset by New Faces – Bedford
Produced by Concept Design Associates – Bedford
Printed by Skeltons Press – Wellingborough

Contents

	(i)	Foreword	7
	(ii)	Preface	9
	(iii)	Acknowledgements	11
Chapter	1.	Introduction	13
Chapter	2.	Computer Equipment	17
Chapter	3.	Word Processing	23
Chapter	4.	Using a Database: A Year File for pupil data	29
Chapter	5.	Options in Physical Education	37
Chapter	6.	Stock Control and Financial Accountability	43
Chapter	7.	Sports Day	49
Chapter	8.	Fitness Work	57
Chapter	9.	Cross Country Race Analysis, Triathlon and Orienteering	67
Chapter	10.	Fixtures, Competition and Results for Various Sport	77
Chapter	11.	Computers as a Teaching Aid	85
Chapter	12.	P.E. Reports and Pupil Profiles	95
		Glossary	101
		Appendix I – P.E. computer programs by Mike Skinsley	105
		Appendix II – other programs	107
		Appendix III – books and courses	109

Where the masculine pronoun occurs it implies that either the masculine or feminine gender applies.

(i)
Foreword
by
David Brodie

Dr. David Brodie who is the Director of the School of Physical Education and Recreation at the University of Liverpool.

The invitation to write the foreword to this book was accepted with pleasure because of the anticipation of a sound, commonsense approach to the use of computers in physical education. I was not disappointed. Mike Skinsley has many years of experience of teaching physical education and he has successfully added his skills and enthusiasm for computing to that experience. This is not a sterile, academic text, but a straightforward, no nonsense book which combines computer technology with good teaching practice. Throughout a strong case is made for using the computer as an adjunct to teaching and thus to permit more time for other activities. Many examples are given which illustrate the increased efficiency to be achieved by using the computer. Its place in the P.E. department may depend on the enthusiasm of staff or the co-operation that can be obtained elsewhere in the school. Whatever decision is made, this book provides and invaluable resource for the P.E. teacher ready to examine the applications of computing in schools.

It is recommended to all those interested in what computers have to offer physical education and Mike Skinsley is to be congratulated for producing such a worthwhile and informative book.

(ii) Preface

It was in October 1982 that I first put my hands on a computer. I bought a Sinclair ZX81 for two reasons. Firstly I wanted my older children to have some experience of using a computer in an increasingly technological world. Secondly, I wanted to explore the possibility that a computer might be able to help with some of the organisational and administrative tasks within my large P.E. department.

It did not take long to realise that computers were fun to use. They *were* able to offer real assistance in some areas of physical education and they provided great satisfaction by solving problems in minutes which previously took me hours to complete.

But there were frustrations too. The tape recorder was a laboriously slow medium for storing data; the memory was too small; the printer was of a poor quality and there was a lack of software related to physical education. Indeed, there was no software except the very primitive games like 'squash' where a 'blob' rebounded off three walls and you had to move a 'bat' across the bottom of the screen to return the ball.

I read books on programming and soon began, by trial and error, to write my own programs. Once I had obained a BBC micro more programming opportunities opened up, due to a better printer, disc storage and a larger memory. Even for the BBC, there were no P.E. programs commercially produced so I had to start writing new programs.

Initially I developed my ideas into single programs for things like fitness testing or options analysis, before I linked many of them around a common 'Year File' which held all the pupils' names – at last, no more writing out of pupil names for each program.

Not only was I using the computer extensively in my department but I also used it to help with some of my other responsibilities in running County schools' sports associations, for instance, for the cross country race analysis at the County Championships.

I also used the computer for some whole school administrative tasks. I adapted my P.E. options program to run the whole of the course choice analysis, for all pupils in Years 4 and 5, when selecting their examination subjects. My P.E. report and pupil profile program has dramatically changed the style of reporting since it has been adopted across the whole school.

Little did I realise how much my life would be changed by writing an article in the Times Educational Supplement (3-2-84) on the subject of using computers in physical education. Within a short time I became involved in running courses for ILEA, national courses for the Physical Education Association, lecturing to university students and giving demonstrations to teachers.

The interaction with fellow members of the P.E. profession during this time has been a great encouragement and a further source of inspiration. I hope this book will inspire others to explore the use of a computer to improve the quality of teaching, administration and organisation in their school.

If only some of the ways in which the computer has enhanced the work in my Physical education department are tried and adopted by the reader, then the writing of this book will have been worthwhile.

Mike Skinsley 1987.

(iii) Acknowledgements

The Physical Education Association without whom this book would not have been published.

Derek Sowden for Artwork (title page) and Photographs 2.1, 2.2, 2.3, 2.4, 8.1, 8.2, 9.1, Front Cover, Rear Cover.

Mike Skinsley Photographs 1.1, 8.3, 10.1.

Peter Skinsley for producing some of the computer material.

Carl Harris for particular encouragement and support.

My Head, P.E. staff and pupils at my school for allowing me the freedom to innovate and experiment with my computerised ideas.

Dr. David Brodie for his professional support and for writing the Foreword.

Sandra Maggs for use of her unpublished thesis on "Microcomputers and Physical Education in the Secondary School" which contained a case study of my department.

Liz, my wife, for reading the manuscript and for her patience and understanding throughout my involvement with computers.

Introduction

"When are we going to use the computer again in P.E., Sir?"

That question by a pupil is not a prediction for the future but the reality of modern day Physical Education. Computers are playing a vital role in assisting physical education teachers with some of their daily tasks.

The computer is a very efficient tool as it is able to handle both written and numerical data, it can save that information and recall it anytime at a later date. The processing of all this data will leave the P.E. teacher and his pupils better informed and in possession of more facts than ever before. The computer can be left to carry out repetitive tasks leaving staff more time to devote to other important matters such as teaching or curriculum planning.

High standards in physical education apply not only to teaching and coaching but also to the administration and organisation of our departmental work. The computer is able to

Picture 1.1

Computer generated material can enhance the appearance of the P.E. notice board.

produce printed material of a very high standard, be it letters, notices or the results of certain analysis, and the P.E. notice board will bear the proof.

Computers are a relatively new innovation in physical education. Many other 'technical' devices have been tried, tested and used to great effect over the years. An account of a school sports day held in 1934 mentioned

"... a great innovation was the amplifier which was used to announce the results."

Other equipment has helped us over the years to improve the quality of our work. This has included the slide projector, the film projector, the record player, the film loop, the overhead projector, cassette tape recorders and the video tape. The computer is simply the latest generation of technical equipment which has now been made available in every school for use by *ALL* teachers.

Computers are not some form of five minute craze like skate boards or hula hoops! The computer is here and it is here to stay. Industry and commerce make extensive use of such technology and education has begun to follow suit. Physical education must be seen to use the computer as much as any other subject in the curriculum so that the needs of our subject will be considered in any future developments.

Everyone will have to become more familiar with the basics of using a computer. Physical education teachers are no exception and they should already be obtaining some practical experience of keyboard skills, It is better to learn how one particular type of computer functions so that it can be used regularly with confidence. Some time will have to be set aside to learn these new skills but it should be regarded as being just as important as attending a course to update ones' knowledge on the teaching of a particular activity.

Introduction

It is a fact that many of our pupils may have more practical experience and knowledge of computers than ourselves. That expertise could be utilised by getting the computer literate pupils to help the P.E. Department. There is no reason why such pupils should not write material, perhaps as part of their computer studies project or assist in the analysis of P.E. data. Pupils unable to take part in practical lessons may be able to operate the computer when it is appropriate.

Computers should not be seen as just the province of the maths or science specialists. Physical educationists have as much right to use computers as anyone else. The computer should also be used just as much by the women P.E. staff and for the girls as by the men P.E. staff and for the boys.

There is no compulsive need for P.E. teachers to know too much technical detail about the inner workings of a computer and it is not the intention of this book to go into too many technical facts. Computers can be used without knowing very much about ROMs, RAMs or REMs, but see the glossary if you are not sure! It is not expected, nor anticipated, that all P.E. teachers will need to become experts in writing their own computer programs. The hope is that P.E. teachers will appreciate and realise the value of using this technology and become frequent users. It is the responsibility of those with the knowledge and expertise in both computers and the needs of physical education to seek out the true potential of these machines for the benefit of all other users.

Having established where the computer can be of most value then suitable programs can be produced. They must not be full of technical jargon but they should contain easy to follow instructions and be adaptable to differing school circumstances. There are many P.E. related computer programs available (see Appendix) which are frequently being used in schools to great effect.

Many other subject areas in the curriculum have had produced for them a large quantity of specially written computer programs whilst physical education has had very little attention from the professional educational program writers. This may be due partly to market forces where it was known that commercially, maths and science would provide a wider market and a more lucrative profit margin.

It would be more advantageous if each Physical Education department could obtain their own computer as part of their general equipment. It may not always be convenient to have to borrow a computer from elsewhere in the school but the investment of a full set of computer equipment would then enable the P.E. department to obtain maximum benefit.

If the computer proves to be a useful tool for the resolving of some of our tasks then it must be used and used regularly. If there is no advantage to be gained in using the computer then normal methods should continue to be practiced.

Although computers are being used in more and more aspects of our daily life it is not the purpose here to look at such applications as the computerised control of the heating, lighting, telephone, cleaners' wages or burglar alarm system for the P.E. block. This book aims to show those areas of teaching and administrative work within physical education which can be significantly improved by using a computer.

Although examples shown in this book are based on a BBC computer, the principles are the same for any other machine. All computers are electronic machines which will manipulate data, both alphabetic and numeric, in a variety of ways. What the computer does with the data depends upon the person who writes the computer programs, the programmer.

So what can a computer do for the P.E. teacher? The computer can carry out many administrative tasks which involve recording, communicating and the processing of information which would normally be committed on to paper. The advantage of using the computer lies in the way in which these tasks are handled. The P.E. teacher has just as much administration to carry out as other teachers. The technology housed within these computers provides systems of operations which are far more efficient and provide a better quality than any previous methods. Even if the computer with a word processor was only used as a replacement for the typewriter then better documents would still emerge. Typewriting skills, whilst useful, are not essential but who knows, perhaps one day, we will be speaking into computers rather than typing in words.

The computer can assist with organisational tasks by handling numbers and making calculations more rapidly and more accurately than could possibly be achieved on paper, even with the aid of a calculator. Unlike most calculators, the computer can be programmed to automatically handle data in particular ways so that hundreds of operations per second will occur. This means that the machine has a great potential when used to analyse scores in a competition, such as on sports day. There is a need in several sports to get results out quickly and organisers of large events could not manage this without the aid of a computer. The pupils should also see the benefits of using this technology by receiving the analysis of results in a fraction of the time previously taken.

The Physical Education teacher will not be replaced by the computer. It is most unlikely that a computer will ever be able to teach a group of children all the finer points of how to play a particular game. Nor are robotic referees likely to take over our whistles. However, P.E. teachers are being seen more often with their hands on a computer to help them with their teaching. The funny looks and sarcastic comments from other staff will soon give way to respect and admiration once the results have been seen.

Computer assisted learning (CAL) in physical education is being used more and more to present facts, rules or strategies of play as part of a programme of work for a particular activity. Sport related 'computer games' have their limitations as far as learning is concerned but they do provide some fun and entertainment. The computer is a valuable additional resource for normal teaching purposes as well as being available for those wet weather days or emergencies.

The computer is a reliable machine which will not tire nor make mistakes, providing the correct information has been entered in the first place. Human error will occur in any aspect of physical education work whether a computer is being used or not. Some of the human errors will be eliminated by using well written computer programs which check whether data being entered is within certain limits or conforms to certain expectations.

The use of a computer in a physical education department has to be worth investigation and evaluation. Those teachers who have ventured into the use of this modern technology have soon discovered the benefits, to their way of working, as well as for their pupils.

Introduction

Computer Equipment

Picture 2.1

A complete set of computer eqiupment for the P.E. Department.

The story of the computer goes back a long way. The abacus is the pre-electronic version of the modern day computer. It was often used, and still is in parts of the world, as a simple yet quick device for handling complex calculations. Pascal built a mechanical calculator as long ago as the mid 1600's which consisted of cogs, gears and rachets but it was only able to carry out the addition of numbers and display the result. Later machines were able to undertake other mathematical calculations and their design was used for nearly three centuries and was still being used to operate shop tills in the 1970's.

A development from the earlier mechanical machines was the valve type 'computer'. In the 1940's these early versions would fill a complete room and need re-wiring to change a program. The appearance of the transistor, followed by the integrated circuits, led to the reduction in size of computers and eventually to a lowering of costs. Successive developments produced computers which were more powerful and faster than the previous generation.

It was not until the early 1970's that the first desk top computers as we know them today arrived. Their appearance is in many respects like the traditional typewriter with a QWERTY keyboard. But there the similarity ends. Many computer programs today run on a menu driven option system which, like the bank cash terminals, prompts the user to press selected buttons at every stage.

To establish a computer system within a P.E. department certain essential pieces of equipment, or computer hardware, will be required. A complete set of equipment consists of four basic items:

a) the computer
b) a screen or monitor
c) a means of storage
d) a printer

THE COMPUTER

The type of computer that a P.E. department would purchase will depend upon how much money is available, the purpose to which it will be put and the availability of suitable computer programs, or software. These three factors have to be considered together before making the final decision.

There is no guarantee that the more expensive the computer the better it will suit your needs. Less expensive machines may be more suitable but beware of obsolete models being sold off very cheaply. There will be a constant up-dating of computer technology so that current models will age and become out of date. Computers may have to be changed every few years if we are to keep abreast of new technological developments.

Some computers will have the ability to attach various essential items (known as peripherals) through various plugs on the machine. Others

Computer Equipment

may need special attachments before items such as printers, disc drives or joy-sticks can be used which will add to the overall cost. When you do buy make sure that all the connecting leads are included as sometimes these come as extras.

Picture 2.2
BBC Computer with a television being used as a monitor.

There is no doubt that the Acorn BBC computer has been the mainstay of educational computers in this country. Other makes of computer, such as the Research Machines 380Z and 480Z and now their Nimbus have also been widely used. All these machines can perform a wide range of tasks and have the ability to use many peripherals. They also have a large number of computer programs immediately available which can be used for educational purposes.

Other computers which offer special word processing packages may be very good for that purpose but may not be suitable for other tasks because very little educational software has

been written. Caution has to be taken before purchase and it is essential to ensure that the computer you wish to buy will accommodate all your needs.

THE SCREEN or MONITOR

By itself a computer is of little use unless it is attached to a screen, monitor or visual display unit (VDU). Many computers can be linked to a normal television set which may reduce costs if you already have access to one. It is better to have the computer connected to a VDU or computer monitor as these have a higher resolution of picture than a television set. This means that the picture is clearer when viewed from the shorter distance. There can be problems when a television is being used as a computer screen and it is needed to watch a school's broadcast.

STORAGE

Material produced on or by the computer may need to be stored and kept for future reference, or for further development. Specially written computer programs do not come as part of the computer hardware (equipment) but are known as software and they have to be on a transportable medium. There are various ways of storing computer data or programs, the most common being on a cassette tape or on a floppy disc. These will need to be used in conjunction with a tape recorder or a disc drive respectively and like computers vary according to their cost.

A standard cassette tape recorder can be linked up to a computer so that programs or data can be transferred to and from normal cassette tapes. The advantage of this system is that it is relatively cheap but that is outweighed by the slowness and restriction of tape as the medium for storage. Information has to be stored sequentially on tape, i.e. one item after another. When this happens it is not possible to find certain bits of information quickly. Any user starting with this system will soon become frustrated by the time it takes to load and save material.

The disc drive has become the more normal method of storing information and the price is now more reasonable. Like the cassette tape the data is stored on a magnetised surface, a flat 'floppy' disc, instead of a thin tape. The disc drive can scan a disc very quickly, find the information required and load it into the computer within seconds compared to the minutes it would take with a cassette recorder.

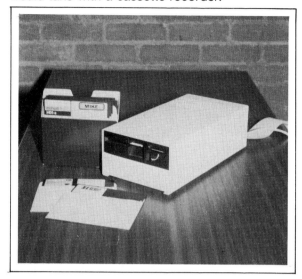

Picture 2.3
A disc drive is used to store computer data.

Care has to be taken when purchasing disc drives as there are various types, again depending on cost. The simplest system would consist of a single drive which would read one side of a 40 track disc. This means that it is a single unit, which can only scan one side of the floppy disc. Each disc has to be 'formatted' to allow data to be stored on either 40 or 80 tracks. Formatting is the way of ordering the magnetised surface of the disc. One side of a 40 track disc can store 100K of data, that is the equivalent of 100,000 single characters of data. An 80 track disc will hold twice as much data. Some disc drives have two units and some can read both sides of a disc. If these drives read 80 track discs then 800K of data can be immediately available or stored at the user's finger tips.

It is a useful precaution to make back-up copies of software or data just in case something goes wrong and using a double disc drive makes copying very much quicker and easier. There is nothing worse than feeding in a lot of information into the computer, storing it, and

then later discovering that the data cannot be read anymore. Care should be taken when handling either tape or discs so as not to touch the magnetised surfaces. This may mean that data stored there cannot be read into the computer.

Some complex computer programs can only operate with double disc drives where the operating disc containing the main program is held in one drive whilst your disc is held in the other for storing information which you generate.

Discs, or tapes can hold so much information that they become very valuable to the user. Great care has to be taken by keeping them in a suitable storage box. It is essential to create a system of knowing what is on each disc or tape. It is best to consider one disc for each P.E. topic, such as one for cross country analysis, another for fitness testing analysis and others for pupil data, etc. Each disc should be clearly labelled and numbered to help in creating a 'library' storage system of the many discs which will quickly develop.

On each disc there will be a number of different files (programs or pieces of data) all of which will need a different identifying name. Part of the fun of using computers can occur from the creation of different names each time you save information. If you continue to use the same name you will simply save over the top of the old file of the same name thereby losing the original. It is usually better to save under a different name and only later erase an earlier version if you are absolutely certain it will no longer be required.

A computer can be made to operate with either tape or disc as the storage medium and simple commands are used to change between the two. There are different types of disc storage, depending upon needs and cost. The most common version is the stand alone disc drive which is only attached to one computer.

There is also the econet system, found in many schools or institutes of higher education, where all the computers in a room can be linked to one master disc storage facility. In this way a computer program can be stored on a master disc and be immediately available to any of the other linked computers. Using a stand alone system every computer would need a separate copy of that program on a different disc, or else

Computer Equipment

one disc would have to be passed around to each user. The stand alone system is perhaps simpler to operate for the non-computer expert than the econet system. It is also more versatile in that computers can be moved around more easily, into the gym for instance, without the need for it to be wired into the econet system which might be housed in a different building. Econet systems normally use a standard 'floppy' disc for the storage of data but there are some systems that operate with a 'hard disc' which can hold considerably more data.

PRINTERS

Computers are frequently used to produce written or numerical data. The monitor may not be a suitable medium to view the whole of the end product, say a long written document, so it will be necessary to commit the final outcome to paper. Computers can consume vast quantities of paper through a connected printer of which there are various types according to needs and cost. Many of the computer printers are so much more versatile than the normal output from a typewriter.

Picture 2.4

A printer which is used in conjunction with the computer.

One form of printer, a dot matrix, forms its letters by means of a series of pins striking a ribbon according to the shape of each character. In draft quality, the letters may not appear very clean as the individual dots can be seen.

However, by printing each line either a second time (double strike) or in a bold format a 'near letter quality' becomes possible. As well as printing letters or numbers these printers can also be used to produce graphics, that is they can reproduce drawings or charts.

Some printers use a daisy wheel head where letters on a rotating wheel are struck against the paper producing a finish of an exceptionally good quality. However, this sort of printer cannot be used for graphs or charts, only for text.

Printers can be fed with individual sheets of paper, or if the work covers many pages, then fan-fold paper is used. This is a continuous form of paper, perforated at the end of each page, which allows the printer to continue with the printing process without the need to keep inserting individual sheets. Fan-folded paper can be obtained in double or treble NCR form which is very useful when printing out results or when a duplicate copy of a letter is required.

It is possible to insert banda or roneo stencils into computer printers to produce further copies if a photocopier is not available. It is inefficient to use a computer printer to reproduce 20 copies of the same set of results but it is a good use to produce 20 copies of the same letter when the computer has individually named and addressed each one.

Printers are available which will reproduce text or diagrams in colour which will add further to the quality and variation in the printed material.

SAFETY

These four main items of computer hardware normally come with their own plugs and inter-connecting wires and cables. This electrical equipment can present a 'health and safety' hazard so care has to be taken to ensure that all wiring is properly installed.

Storage and movement of computer equipment must also be considered. Computers do not like being in a damp atmosphere so storage or use where there might be condensa-tion, from the changing room showers for instance, should be avoided. If computers have to be moved about, the ideal solution is to keep it all on a trolley and wheel it into the gym or sports hall when required. Remember to avoid moving the equipment through the changing rooms when showers are taking place at the end of the lesson.

OTHER CONSIDERATIONS

Using computers will enhance the work of any P.E. department. The P.E. teacher will be rewarded with a great deal of satisfaction and pride as a result of his efforts. However, there will be times of frustration. Some will occur, as mentioned earlier, because of the time it takes to load material from tape before being able to use a particular program. Frustrations will occur when programs may not quite carry out the tasks which you would like them to do, especially when you do not have the knowledge or ability to alter the program yourself.

A lack of compatibility between equipment or programs can be extremely frustrating. Many computers understand a 'basic' language but different makes of computers have slight varia-tions in their basic language. As a result a program for one computer will not run on a computer of another make.

Even the same make of computers change their technology as they are updated. The BBC has developed through from the model 'A' to a 'B', then a 'B+', an 'Electron', the Master and the Compact. They contain different up-dated forms of 'basic' and some have different types of disc filing systems. The BBC is no exception in this respect as it also happens with other manufacturers. It reinforces the probability that we will have to change our computers every few years to keep up with modern developments.

USING COMPUTERS

Like the games and activities we teach, learning to become familiar with computers will need much practice. Many training courses are available but some might be too technical dealing only with programming. A more practical based course giving hands on experience would be more appropriate for beginners. (See Appendix III for information on P.E. based computer courses).

Manuals which accompany computer equipment can either be great sources of help and information or be totally incomprehensible unless you have a higher degree in computing. You may have to purchase other books

associated with your computer or subscribe to one of the many magazines to broaden your knowledge of these machines. Above all, practice will widen your skills and ability, providing you are willing and prepared to learn from your mistakes that will inevitably occur in your early days.

Contact with other users of computers can be a further source of help and assistance. This help might be forthcoming from the computer studies staff or by meeting with other physical education teachers who are also using computers in their departments. The latter is particularly valuable to exchange ideas and opinions on suitable software for physical educa-tion.

Like any other machine breakdowns may happen to a computer. It is useful to know who you can call upon or where you can go to obtain help in repairing or sorting out anything which might go wrong. Do not leave it until it is too late. Finding out this information will avoid a panic situation occurring if there are technical problems on the morning of your cross country champion-ships when you are analysing the results on the computer!

Computer Equipment

Word Processing

Physical Education notices or letters used to appear, and in some cases still do, in one of three forms. Firstly there were the hand written ones, some neater than others. This was done for pure speed but only if the material was relatively short and if only one copy was required.

Secondly there were the Banda produced documents which came in a variety of hews, from the very faint to the very blue, from the very smudged to that rare specimen, a very clear copy. This depended on how hard the user pressed on the master and how proficient the teacher was at operating the Banda machine. Mistakes were always impossible to remove on both of these methods and frequently the letter would have to be re-written, especially if it was an important circular to parents or to the head.

Lastly the Roneo stencil provided a better quality of duplicated material and had the added advantage that any mistake could be blotted out with correction fluid and then re-typed over the top. To produce this form of notice or letter the material had to be written out in long hand and handed to the school secretary for typing and duplication. This could take the office staff one or two days to complete, or even longer, depending on how busy they were. With the arrival of a photocopier, the banda and roneo methods of duplication could be phased out. However, even with a photo-copier letters might still stay in the office tray for several days before they are typed, checked and printed.

Now that computers are more readily available in schools, all teachers, including P.E. teachers, should be using word processors for all their written material. The word processor is more efficient in the long term and produces a far better quality of print out than previous traditional methods. Ultimately, when a P.E. department obtains their own computer equipment with a word processor, they can produce any written material directly themselves, whenever and however they want it.

In appearance, part of a modern computer resembles the type writer with its similar and familiar keyboard. The technology which has gone into the making of the computer has produced a very versatile machine which provides, amongst other things, a much improved version of the typewriter.

By itself however, the computer will not perform very well as a 'type writing machine' but by adding a word processing facility the computer is transformed into a very efficient, effective and clever writing tool. Word processing is only possible by permanently inserting an extra 'chip' into the computer (like Wordwise or View) or by using a disc based version of a word processing program (like Mini Office).

The word processor has revolutionised the writing and typing of material. Words can be entered into the computer just as on a typewriter but there the similarities end. Several features are available in a word processor which are not possible with the type writer. The user is given a choice of various procedures which would appear as a menu of options as shown below. They will include an ability to –

1. Save text.
2. Load text previously saved.
3. Preview written text on the screen as it would appear in print.
4. Print the text, i.e. send all the text to the printer.
5. A search and replace facility.
6. An editing mode.

All of the writing is carried out in an editing mode where there is no need to worry about text overlapping at the end of a line as the word processor automatically adjusts each line accordingly.

Word Processing

Codes or markers can be used to create different features in the text. For instance, as on a typewriter, a left or right margin can be set but special features such as the right justification of text is only possible with a word processor.

Sections can be marked and then copied elsewhere or moved to another part of the document. Mistakes are easily corrected. Single letters, whole words or whole sections of text can be quickly deleted. Letters or words can be inserted or over-written and the text will once more adjust itself automatically. A search and replace facility allows the user to change words or names throughout the whole document.

Some word processors will show the text on the screen in the way it will appear on paper, 80 characters wide. Others may show the text in editing mode in a 40 character wide format with an option to preview the text to check the layout before printing commences. Further alterations may then be necessary in the editing mode. Throughout all the writing or editing the computer shows the total number of words which have been written to give the user an accurate indication of the length.

The approved version of the written material can be saved on disc for future use or reference. Letters or documents can be partly written, stored on disc and then loaded back at a later date for completion. Similar letters can be recalled and then amended instead of being completely re-typed at a later date. This is why the word processor is rated so highly as an efficient writing tool. Material can be stored from one year to the next, and within minutes a new version can be ready for the photocopier with no need to re-draft or wait for it to be re-typed.

Once satisfied with a document, the text can be directed to the printer for a hard copy to be produced on paper. Various commands can be inserted into the text to produce different types of printing effects. Larger (enlarged) or smaller (condensed) print can be obtained from dot matrix printers, or a heavier print (bold and/or double strike) for a better quality of finish and clarity. Some dot matrix printers claim to produce a finish of NLQ or Near Letter Quality. This is where the action of the pins in the printer head produce a more 'solid' finish to each letter, similar to a normal typewriter. Some computer printers use a daisy wheel head which gives a better quality of print than a dot matrix printer but the daisy wheel printers are not able to produce a print out of any graphics material.

If many copies are needed then a photo copier can be used to reproduce the required number from the original word processed document. It is even possibie to insert Banda or Roneo skin into the computer printer if these methods of duplication are the only ones available.

These are just some of the features available in a word proessor package and with practice the user can quickly become a very proffificent operator. So much so that it may become quicker and easier for the teacher to produce his own type-written material rather than draft it out long hand and submit it to the school office.

Within a P.E. department there are a number of events which occur annually which necessitate a letter being circulated around staff and pupils. These will include notices concerning various inter house or inter tutor group competitions, such as cross country, football, hockey or swimming. (See Figure 3.1). In the examples shown there is unlikely to be a major change or

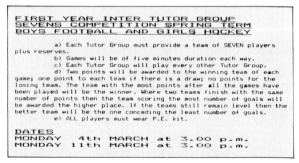

Figure 3.1
Example of word processed competition notice.

format or rules from one year to the next. The only changes will be the day and date of the events.

After typing these documents into the word processor they should be stored on disc so that they can be recalled the following year. It only takes seconds to return the letter into the computer and within a very short time the new dates can be inserted. The new version can be ready and printed out in minutes and be ready for photo copying in the time it would take to re-draft the letter by hand in readiness for a secretary to type out.

There are additional benefits when material is generated on a word processor. Parts of one document can be taken and used as part of another. For instance, on the notice concerning the inter house swimming gala, (Figure 3.2) all

```
        INTER  HOUSE  SWIMMING  GALA

        Inter House Swimming Galas will be held for Years 1, 2 and 3
as follows :
        1st Years  Monday 13th May    at 3.00 p.m.
        2nd Years  Monday 29th April at 3.00 p.m.
        3rd Years  Monday 22nd April at 3.00 p.m.

        For the individual events each House requires 2 pupils for
each race. For the Relay races each House requires 4 pupils in each
team. A Medley team shall consist of one backstroke swimmer, one
breast stroke swimmer, one butterfly swimmer and one front crawl
swimmers.

        Each pupil may enter ONE individual event, plus the
Butterfly, plus ONE Relay.
```

GIRLS 4 X 1 LENGTH MEDLEY RELAY	'	'	'	'
BOYS 4 X 1 LENGTH MEDLEY RELAY	'	'	'	'
GIRLS 1 LENGTH BREAST STROKE	'	'		
BOYS 1 LENGTH BREAST STROKE	'	'		
GIRLS 1 LENGTH BACK STROKE	'	'		
BOYS 1 LENGTH BACK STROKE	'	'		
GIRLS 1 LENGTH BUTTERFLY	'	'		
BOYS 1 LENGTH BUTTERFLY	'	'		
GIRLS 1 LENGTH FREESTYLE	'	'		
BOYS 1 LENGTH FREESTYLE	'	'		
GIRLS 4 X 1 LENGTH FREESTYLE RELAY	'	'	'	'
BOYS 4 X 1 LENGTH FREESTYLE RELAY	'	'	'	'

Figure 3.2
Details for the Swimming Gala.

the events have to be listed and in this case spaces have also been provided for team managers to insert the names of competitors. On the day, competitors will need to know the order of events and so it is possible to extract the list of events from the first document and produce a new sheet showing the order of events (Figure 3.3) without having to re-write that list again. The word processor could be used to produce the whole of a much larger Swimming Gala Programme for spectators which might include the names of competitors, the teams competing, the officials, points scored, trophies to be won and the dates of future events as well as the order of events.

Every P.E. Department should produce an annual Handbook of information about itself. Such a Handbook would contain details about the school, the Departmental aims and objectives, a breakdown of the curriculum, a list of responsibilities held by the various members of the Department and the procedures and rules to be observed. This is likely to be a substantial document but few Departments produce one mainly because of the time involved in writing,

```
INTER  HOUSE  SWIMMING  GALA

ORDER  OF  EVENTS

 1.   GIRLS 4 X 1 LENGTH MEDLEY RELAY
 2.   BOYS  4 X 1 LENGTH MEDLEY RELAY

 3.   GIRLS 1 LENGTH BREAST STROKE
 4.   BOYS  1 LENGTH BREAST STROKE

 5.   GIRLS 1 LENGTH BACK STROKE
 6.   BOYS  1 LENGTH BACK STROKE

 7.   GIRLS 1 LENGTH BUTTERFLY
 8.   BOYS  1 LENGTH BUTTERFLY

 9.   GIRLS 1 LENGTH FREESTYLE
10.   BOYS  1 LENGTH FREESTYLE

11.   GIRLS 4 X 1 LENGTH FREESTYLE RELAY
12.   BOYS  4 X 1 LENGTH FREESTYLE RELAY
```

Figure 3.3
Part of the Swimming Gala details have been used to create the order of events for the Gala Programme.

updating and getting it typed each year. The word processor will handle such a document with ease and once it has been written and saved on disc it then becomes a very easy task to up-date, add to, alter or amend each year.

Normally when using a word proccessor any document will be printed out in a continuous format. However, a long document can be split into separate pages when it is printed by inserting special commands which puts the computer into a paged mode. These commands are written into the text but do not appear in print as they have to be inserted between embedded commands. Extra sections or paragraphs can be added or deleted and the computer will automatically adjust the document, page by page. A heading can be printed on each page either at the top or the bottom as well as the automatic numbering of the pages.

For the technically minded the embedded commands would be similar to this list depending upon the word processor. These are the commands used in the Wordwise Plus or Mini Office word processors.

    1. Enable paging. (EP)
    2. Set left margin to 5 spaces. (LM5)
    3. Let there be 4 spaces at the top of the page. (TS4)
    4. Let there be 4 spaces at the bottom of each page. (BS4)
    5. If the user wants double spacing set the

Word Processing

line space to two. (LS2)

6. Set the page length to 60 lines. (PL60)
7. Set the line length to 70 characters. (LL70)
8. Define the heading which might be centred (CE) across the page and underlined. (US and UE)
9. Some word processors, like Wordwise Plus, will automatically insert the word PAGE and the page number once paging has been enabled but in others the user has to set this command.

Using Wordwise Plus the command for this format would be entered as shown below. At the beginning of a document *WORD PROCESSING* will appear in the centre at the top of each page and the page number at the bottom. «f1» or «f2» indicates where the user would press the function keys 1 or 2 to start or end the embedded commands.

«f1»EP«f1»LM5«f1»TS4«f1»BS4«f1»LS2«f1»PL60 «f1»DH«f1»CE«f2» «f1»US«f2»WORD PROCES-SING«f1»UE«f2»

(NOTE: one SPACE must be inserted between «f1»CE«f2» and «f1»US«f2»).

This might appear complicated and it may take several attempts to find the most suitable format for particular documents. Once the best formula has been found then the heading should be saved for use at any time with any other document or booklet.

Some computers have an ability to program certain 'function keys' on the computer. The commands listed above, and others, could be automatically fed into these function keys each time the user used the word processor. Then, if a certain format was required, the user could quickly enter the commands into the text from these pre-programmed function keys.

Here is a short and simple BASIC program which would program the function keys 1 to 4 on a BBC computer which contained Wordwise Plus.

```
10 *KEY1«f1»EP«f1»LM5«f1»TS4«f1»BS4«f1»
   LS2«f1»PL60«f1»DH«f1»CE«f2»
   «f1»US«f2»WORD PROCESSING«f1»
   UE«f2»
20 *KEY2«f1»US«f2»
30 *KEY3«f1»UE«f2»
40 *KEY4«f1»CE«f2»
50 *WORDWISE
```

You would need to save this program on disc, then RUN the program and it would set up the function keys 1 to 4 and select the word processor chip. Starting a new document the user enters the paging formula by pressing SHIFT/CTRL and function key f1. Keys 2, 3 and 4 will allow the user to enter the individual commands to start underlining, to end underlining and to centre respectively.

The word processing system is extremely useful for anyone who is responsible for running a County Sports Association or a District team. During each year many letters have to be circulated which are the same or very similar to the ones sent out the previous year. In cross country for instance, it might be necessary to contact athletes, teachers, Heads or Club Officials some twenty times during a season with circulars like figure 3.4.

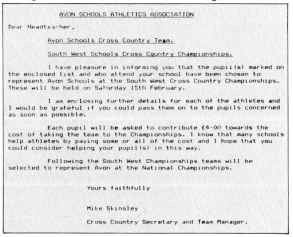

Figure 3.4
One of many County letters produced with the word processor then saved on disc for recall and amendment the following year.

Once these twenty different documents have been produced on the word processor they can be recalled annually and changes can be quickly made to items such as the date, venue and cost of travel.

The word processor can also be used for producing team lists and results and although it may initially take a short while to set up a desired format, once created the system can be used very efficiently year after year. Figure 3.5 shows a team list for a county cross

```
! AVON SCHOOLS JUNIOR BOYS CROSS          !
! COUNTRY TEAM FOR S.W. CHAMPS 1986        !
!------------------------------------------!
! No.! NAME              ! SCHOOL          !
!----!-------------------!-----------------!
!  1 ! RICHARD HADLEY    ! CLEVEDON        !
!  2 ! DARREN BANCROFT   ! CASTLE          !
!  3 ! TIM ARTUS         ! ST. GEORGE      !
!  4 ! PAUL ORCHARD      ! CHIPPING SODBURY!
!  5 ! EDWARD RAYMOND    ! TOCKINGTON MANOR!
!  6 ! MARCUS STEELE     ! HENGROVE        !
!  7 ! PAUL BRISTOW      ! BRISLINGTON     !
!  8 ! PETER WYATT       ! BACKWELL        !
!  9 ! JOHN BOUGHTON     ! MONKS PARK      !
! 10 ! NICK HASKINS      ! MANGOTSFIELD    !
!------------------------------------------!
! RESERVES                                 !
!------------------------------------------!
! 11 ! SIMON PEARCE      ! TOCKINTON MANOR !
! 12 ! NICHOLAS JUDD     ! THE GRANGE      !
! 13 ! STEPHEN SLOCOMBE  ! HENGROVE        !
! 14 ! STEPHEN ROSE      ! CULVERHAY       !
! 15 ! DANIEL NOAD       ! CULVERHAY       !
! 16 ! LEE BILLINGHAM    ! PRIORY          !
!------------------------------------------!


! AVON SCHOOLS INTERMEDIATE BOYS CROSS     !
! COUNTRY TEAM FOR S.W. CHAMPS 1986        !
!------------------------------------------!
! No.! NAME              ! SCHOOL          !
!----!-------------------!-----------------!
!  1 ! IAN GILLESPIE     ! ST. BEDES       !
!  2 ! JAMES HOLBROOK    ! DOWNEND         !
!  3 ! RICHARD CRANSWICK ! THE CASTLE      !
!  4 ! OLIVER PRATT      ! BACKWELL        !
!  5 ! VINCENT PUGSLEY   ! SIR BERNARD LOVELL!
!  6 ! JEFFERY STARKEY   ! BRISLINGTON     !
!  7 ! MATTHEW HICKS     ! THE GRANGE      !
!  8 ! LANCE WOODHAM     ! CULVERHAY       !
!  9 ! CARL CAINES       ! SPEEDWELL       !
! 10 ! KEVIN SAGE        ! MONKS PARK      !
!------------------------------------------!
! RESERVES                                 !
!------------------------------------------!
! 11 ! ANDREW EADIE      ! MONKTON COMBE   !
! 12 ! RICHARD SHEARER   ! PRIORY          !
! 13 ! PETER DODGE       ! KING EDWARDS    !
! 14 ! ALEX LAVIS        ! MARLWOOD        !
! 15 ! MARCUS BROWNING   ! HARTCLIFFE      !
! 16 ! RUPERT WHITAKER   ! PRIOR PARK COLLEGE!
!------------------------------------------!
```

Figure 3.5
A neat, clear design for the County Teams.

```
!------------------------------------------!
! AVON SCHOOLS JUNIOR BOYS CROSS           !
! COUNTRY RESULTS FOR S.W. CHAMPS 1986     !
!------------------------------------------!
! Pos! NAME              ! SCHOOL          !
!----!-------------------!-----------------!
!  1 ! DARREN BANCROFT   ! CASTLE          !
!  3 ! RICHARD HADLEY    ! CLEVEDON        !
! 12 ! TIM ARTUS         ! ST. GEORGE      !
! 13 ! PAUL BRISTOW      ! BRISLINGTON     !
! 18 ! PAUL ORCHARD      ! CHIPPING SODBURY!
! 28 ! EDWARD RAYMOND    ! TOCKINGTON MANOR!
! 39 ! PETER WYATT       ! BACKWELL        !
! 40 ! SIMON PEARCE      ! TOCKINTON MANOR !
! 56 ! NICK HASKINS      ! MANGOTSFIELD    !
!------------------------------------------!
! TEAM 75 POINTS   2nd PLACE               !
!------------------------------------------!
```

Figure 3.6
With the word processor the Team list can quickly be converted into the Result Sheet.

'No.' became Pos, 'RESERVES' became the team points and place whilst the six reserves were deleted. Using a combination of over-write for the positions and movement of marked text for the names of competitors and their schools, the results can be printed out remarkably quickly.

Corresponding between a number of schools could be carried out using an electronic mailing system. Using a 'modem' which links a computer with the telephone line, data can be transmitted to a computer in another school, providing they too have a modem. Letters could be sent for the attention of the P.E. teacher and they would be received and printed out within minutes of being sent. Any reply could be returned with similar rapidity. Fixture arranging via an electronic mailing system could be carried out very quickly providing all schools had the equipment.

There may be a need to produce work sheets for certain physical education lessons, either as part of our curriculum work or perhaps for those occasions when staff are absent or when facilities are not available. It is much better if these worksheets or sports questions are produced on the word processor and saved as before. (Figure 3.7) Even exercises such as word searches can be designed and produced on the word processor. (Figure 3.8).

There are now computer programs which will enable written work generated on a word processor to be wrapped around related graphics

country event. Using the over-write mode new names and schools can be quickly inserted over the previous years names whilst still retaining the basic format.

Figure 3.6 shows how one of the team lists was altered very slightly to enable the same format to be used for a result sheet. Changes were made so that 'team' became 'result',

Word Processing

```
                    SPORTS QUIZ
  1.  Name the four main strokes in swimming.
  2.  In which sport would you use a puck?
  3.  How many points are scored for a try in rugby union?
  4.  A referee for football but an _____ in cricket.
  5.  How many points is the pink ball worth in snooker?
  6.  In athletics name four jumps.
  7.  How many players in a hockey team?
  8.  What is hit over the net in Badminton?
  9.  Name two sports where slalom poles are used.
 10.  Write down names of sports or terms used in sport beginning with
      the letter 'B'.
```

Figure 3.7
*If worksheets are produced on a word processor they can be
easily changed for different age groups without completely
re-typing.*

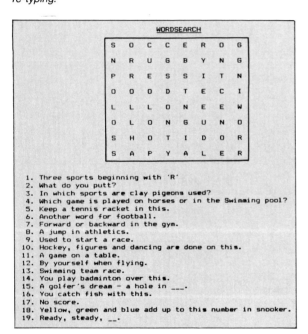

```
                    WORDSEARCH
           S   O   C   C   E   R   O   G
           N   R   U   G   B   Y   N   G
           P   R   E   S   S   I   T   N
           O   O   O   D   T   E   C   I
           L   L   L   O   N   E   E   W
           O   L   O   N   G   U   N   O
           S   H   O   T   I   D   O   R
           S   A   P   Y   A   L   E   R
```

 1. Three sports beginning with 'R'
 2. What do you putt?
 3. In which sports are clay pigeons used?
 4. Which game is played on horses or in the Swimming pool?
 5. Keep a tennis racket in this.
 6. Another word for football.
 7. Forward or backward in the gym.
 8. A jump in athletics.
 9. Used to start a race.
10. Hockey, figures and dancing are done on this.
11. A game on a table.
12. By yourself when flying.
13. Swimming team race.
14. You play badminton over this.
15. A golfer's dream - a hole in ___.
16. You catch fish with this.
17. No score.
18. Yellow, green and blue add up to this number in snooker.
19. Ready, steady, __.

Figure 3.8
A word search design is easy with a word processor.

Figure 3.9
*With added graphics worksheets can be made to look more
interesting.*

There is no doubt that by using a word processor
the quality of any written material will be raised
quite significantly. A great deal of time will also
be saved over the years once the system has
been set up.

material. These graphics can be extracted from a
'library' of pictures or even created by the user,
although the latter does take time. Different page
formats are possible as are different sizes of text
and graphics. The resulting page is certainly
more interesting and attractive than the ordinary
version. Pupils may pay more attention to the
work required of them when the standard of
presentation is more up to date and exciting to
look at. (Figure 3.9).

The quality of our written material is just as
important as the quality of our practical work.

Using a Database:
A Year File for Pupil Data

A database or an information retrieval program is one which can store information, manipulate and sort the data according to certain requirements and then print out the results. Such operations are performed very quickly and with great accuracy, providing the original data has been entered correctly.

A database program might be used to catalogue all the P.E. books in the department or hold the school records for Sports Day. In principle it is like storing information in a filing cabinet or in a card index system. The problem with filing cabinets is that sometimes items are put in the wrong file. Some items may qualify for more than one file so consequently much time

may be spent searching through several files until the item is found.

To create a card record system of all the P.E. books in our department three separate indexes would need to be written out to provide a thorough reference system. Books would be listed as in figure 4.1 under –
 1. alphabetical order by author
 2. alphabetical order by book title
 3. alphabetical order by activity

A book could be found by looking through the appropriate index, depending upon whether it is the author, the title or the activity that is known. A computer database avoids the duplication of

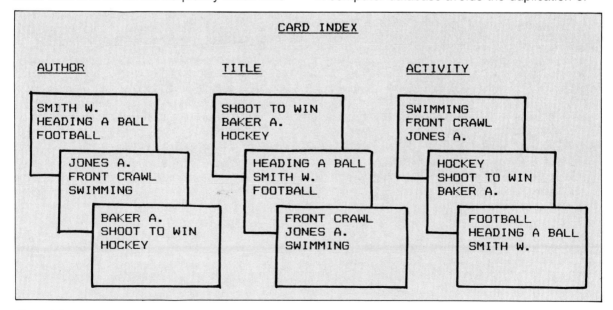

Figure 4.1
A card index filing system for P.E. library books.

Using a Database

the card index system by storing only one copy of the details of each book. Given only part of the information about a book the computer can be asked to carry out a search to find all the remaining details of the required book.

The computer can be asked to list all the books alphabetically by author (figure 4.2), by title (figure 4.3) or by activity (figure 4.4) from the one set of data. This information will be displayed on the computer screen and does not have to be printed out on paper unless requested. The computer can be asked to identify all books on a specific activity and four books have been found in the list related to "Hockey" (figure 4.5). Perhaps only part of the information about a book, such as the author of a book was known to be "Jones" can be remembered. In this case the computer can be made to identify all those books whose author was called "Jones". (Figure 4.6). A database will be able to search all the records and display those which match a certain combination of criteria. By defining that the author is called "Jones" and that the activity is related to "swimming" then the computer in its search will find only one title, that of "Front Crawl" by Jones A.

The library book example is a simple demonstration of the use of a database or information retrieval package. A P.E. teacher can use a database in many different ways to help with the administrative tasks of running a department and many examples will appear throughout the book.

```
P.E. LIBRARY BOOKS
------------------
ALPHABETICAL BY TITLE
------------------------

TITLE              AUTHOR      ACTIVITY
-----------------------------------------------
BETTER DEFENDING   BROWN M     HOCKEY
BOUNCE WITH ME     FORD B      TRAMPOLINING
FASTER RUNNING     FRANK T     ATHLETICS
FIT AND FAST       HILL K      ATHLETICS
FRONT CRAWL        JONES A     SWIMMING
GOALKEEPING        CREST P     HOCKEY
HEADING A BALL     SMITH W     FOOTBALL
HIT THE NET        SKY G       FOOTBALL
PASS THE BALL      STEAD D     RUGBY
POWER AND GRACE    DRING S     GYMNASTICS
SHOOT TO WIN       BAKER A     HOCKEY
SUPER DRIBBLE      JONES G     HOCKEY
```

Figure 4.3
The database list of books by Title.

```
P.E. LIBRARY BOOKS
------------------
ALPHABETICAL BY ACTIVITY
--------------------------

ACTIVITY       TITLE            AUTHOR
-----------------------------------------------
ATHLETICS      FASTER RUNNING   FRANK T
ATHLETICS      FIT AND FAST     HILL K
FOOTBALL       HEADING A BALL   SMITH W
FOOTBALL       HIT THE NET      SKY G
GYMNASTICS     POWER AND GRACE  DRING S
HOCKEY         BETTER DEFENDING BROWN M
HOCKEY         GOALKEEPING      CREST P
HOCKEY         SHOOT TO WIN     BAKER A
HOCKEY         SUPER DRIBBLE    JONES G
RUGBY          PASS THE BALL    STEAD D
SWIMMING       FRONT CRAWL      JONES A
TRAMPOLINING   BOUNCE WITH ME   FORD B
```

Figure 4.4
The database list of books by Activity.

```
P.E. LIBRARY BOOKS
------------------
ALPHABETICAL BY AUTHOR
------------------------

AUTHOR      TITLE             ACTIVITY
-----------------------------------------------
BAKER A     SHOOT TO WIN      HOCKEY
BROWN M     BETTER DEFENDING  HOCKEY
CREST P     GOALKEEPING       HOCKEY
DRING S     POWER AND GRACE   GYMNASTICS
FORD B      BOUNCE WITH ME    TRAMPOLINING
FRANK T     FASTER RUNNING    ATHLETICS
HILL K      FIT AND FAST      ATHLETICS
JONES A     FRONT CRAWL       SWIMMING
JONES G     SUPER DRIBBLE     HOCKEY
SKY G       HIT THE NET       FOOTBALL
SMITH W     HEADING A BALL    FOOTBALL
STEAD D     PASS THE BALL     RUGBY
```

Figure 4.2
The database list of books by Author.

```
P.E. LIBRARY BOOKS ON HOCKEY
------------------------------

AUTHOR      TITLE             ACTIVITY
-----------------------------------------------
BAKER A     SHOOT TO WIN      HOCKEY
BROWN M     BETTER DEFENDING  HOCKEY
CREST P     GOALKEEPING       HOCKEY
JONES G     SUPER DRIBBLE     HOCKEY
```

Figure 4.5
The database will locate all books on any single activity.

```
┌─────────────────────────────────────────────┐
│ P.E. LIBRARY BOOKS WRITTEN BY "JONES"         │
│ --------------------------------------------- │
│ AUTHOR          TITLE            ACTIVITY      │
│ --------------------------------------------- │
│ JONES A         FRONT CRAWL      SWIMMING      │
│ JONES G         SUPER DRIBBLE    HOCKEY        │
└─────────────────────────────────────────────┘
```

Figure 4.6
The database will locate all books from a single or multiple query.

The structure of a database, that is the way the information is organised, is determined by the user. Both written and numerical data can be processed in a database so the use of such a program has endless possibilities. The storing of frequently used data, such as pupil names allows that information to be recalled at any time thereby avoiding the need to keep writing out those same details.

The school office traditionally kept all pupil data in a book but now many schools are using a computer database instead. Such programs can easily handle the vast amount of essential data about each pupil.

Various database programs are available on the market, all of which are designed to store, manipulate and print out data as required. Up to twenty different pieces of information might be stored about each pupil which will include items such as admission number, date of admission, date of leaving, first names, surname, tutor group, house, date of birth, address, telephone number, parents and their contact telephone number, feeder school and sex. Space can be allocated for test results, examination course choices and examination entries. The database can be quickly and easily up-dated and staff can obtain copies of all or a selection of the pupil data.

There are many occasions when physical education teachers need some of this data about pupils but obviously not all of it. For example, lists of pupil's names are needed during cross country races, when carrying out fitness tests or when running and analysing P.E. options.

Ideally, information stored in the main school administration program could be made available on disc for use in analysis programs for physical education. Unfortunately that may not be possible for several reasons.

Sometimes the administration computer may be a different make of computer from the computer which is available to the P.E. staff. Different computers do not "talk" to each other so transfering data from one to another may not be possible.

It is also unlikely that the pupil data which was created in a program produced by one software writer will be stored in such a way that it could be used in another P.E. computer program which has been produced by a different software writer. This lack of compatability between computer hardware and/or computer software can be a problem and is very frustrating at times.

The solution is to have a suite of programs specially written for the P.E. specialist so that pupil data created in one program can be used in several others. A simple Year File program for physical education needs to contain only a few items of information about each pupil.

This basic information about each pupil can be typed into a Year File, a database type program, then saved onto a disc where it can then be used by other compatible P.E. computer programs. In this way the user will only 'write' pupil names ONCE into the computer when the pupils first enter the school. There should be no need to write out those names again during the next five years!

The essential elements of pupil data that need recording are

1. Christian name
2. Surname
3. Tutor group
4. House
5. Sex.

In addition to these five items each pupil would be allocated a reference number as it is quicker to access data from the computer about a pupil by entering a reference number than by having to type out the full name each time.

Entry of each pupil record is very quick. The reference number is automatically selected by the computer whilst the pupils names are the only items to be entered in full. The Tutor Group, House names and gender are entered as a number as illustrated in figure 4.7.

Using a Database

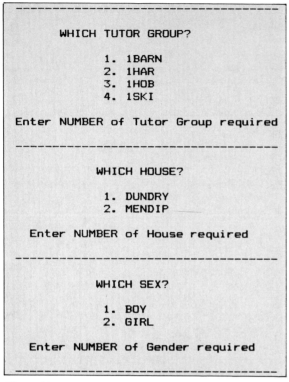

```
--------------------------------------------

        WHICH TUTOR GROUP?


              1.  1BARN
              2.  1HAR
              3.  1HOB
              4.  1SKI

Enter NUMBER of Tutor Group required

--------------------------------------------


        WHICH HOUSE?


              1.  DUNDRY
              2.  MENDIP

    Enter NUMBER of House required

--------------------------------------------


        WHICH SEX?


              1.  BOY
              2.  GIRL

    Enter NUMBER of Gender required

--------------------------------------------
```

Figure 4.7
A quick, numerical entry for Tutor Group, House and Gender information, all part of the Year File data.

```
YEAR FILE - REFERENCE NUMBER LIST

001  JAMIE           CROSS        BARN  DUNDRY  B
002        KAREN     FRY          BARN  DUNDRY  G
003  STEVEN          HARVEY       BARN  MENDIP  B
004        TRACEY    HATHAWAY     BARN  MENDIP  G
005  DAVID           HUGHES       BARN  DUNDRY  B
006        SHARON    MIZEN        BARN  DUNDRY  G
007  GERRY           VOLLERO      BARN  MENDIP  B
008        TINA      WEST         BARN  MENDIP  G
009        LISA      BEDFORD      HAR   MENDIP  G
010  ANDREW          BUSH         HAR   MENDIP  B
011        CAROLINE  FOX          HAR   DUNDRY  G
012  JEFFREY         GAMAN        HAR   DUNDRY  B
013        LISA      HOWARD       HAR   MENDIP  G
014  ANDREW          LEWIS        HAR   MENDIP  B
015        JANE      NOTTON       HAR   DUNDRY  G
016  DARREN          SUTTON       HAR   DUNDRY  B
017  MICHAEL         EDGAR        HOB   MENDIP  B
018        NICOLA    GRANGER      HOB   MENDIP  G
019        JULIE     HILL         HOB   DUNDRY  G
020        TRACEY    MEACHAM      HOB   MENDIP  G
021        MANDY     OXENHAM      HOB   DUNDRY  G
022  PAUL            RUSH         HOB   DUNDRY  B
023  KEITH           THOMPSON     HOB   MENDIP  B
024  PAUL            WAGLAND      HOB   DUNDRY  B
025        KATHERINE BARNES       SKI   DUNDRY  G
026  DAVID           BARRINGTON   SKI   DUNDRY  B
027  DONALD          FORD         SKI   MENDIP  B
028        TANIA     FORD         SKI   MENDIP  G
029        DEBORAH   HAWKES       SKI   DUNDRY  G
030  SHANE           HOBBS        SKI   DUNDRY  B
031  NEIL            PAYNE        SKI   MENDIP  B
032        LISA      WATKINS      SKI   MENDIP  G

NUMBER OF BOYS  = 16
NUMBER OF GIRLS = 16
TOTAL           = 32
```

Figure 4.8
An imaginary Year Group which has been entered into the 'Year File'.

The computer actually stores much of the data numerically to save space and an individual record for Harry Smith in tutor group 1HOB and in MENDIP house will look like this:

037	HARRY SMITH	03021

037 is the reference number for HARRY SMITH. The first two digits (03) refer to the third tutor group, HOB.
The third and fourth digits (02) refer to the second house, MENDIP.
The last digit (1) in this case stands for a boy, whilst a 2 would be a girl.

Figure 4.8 shows a 'Year Group' of 32 pupils listed, as it was entered, in reference number order and also in Tutor Group order. It shows their reference number, christian and surname, their tutor group (mnemonics of the teachers – BARN, HAR, HOB, SKI), their Houses (local hills – DUNDRY and MENDIP) and their gender. To help in the identification of boys and girls, the names have been offset and totals of each shown at the bottom.

As soon as the last of these names has been entered the data is saved on disc using a title such as 'YEAR1' since it contains an up to date whole Year File in reference number order of that year group. Higher up the school this whole year type of record would be used for the anlaysis of Options as part of the P.E. program for both boys and girls. These year files could also be used for inserting pupil names into a P.E. reports program.

The computer can sort out these names in several other ways, display them on the monitor, save the new order on disc and print the revised list on to paper.

The surnames of all pupils can be sorted

alphabetically (figure 4.9) and saved as '1ALPHA'. This file can then be used in the options program if the lists are preferred in alphabetical order rather than tutor group order. It would also be needed when other group lists are required in alphabetical order as opposed to reference number order.

An alphabetical list of each tutor group (figure 4.10) is obtained after first completing a full year alphabetical sort. Similarly, each House group can be identified in this way. (Figure 4.11).

The Tutor Groups or House groups can be saved individually, as '1SKI' or '1DUNDRY' respectively. This kind of sort will produce lists which when printed would help the P.E. teacher in sorting out teaching groups. These lists would be useful in themselves for tutors or for house staff by providing them with a full alphabetical list of all their pupils. Such a list could then help

```
YEAR FILE - ALPHABETIC LIST

025       KATHERINE BARNES       SKI  DUNDRY  G
026  DAVID          BARRINGTON   SKI  DUNDRY  B
009       LISA      BEDFORD      HAR  MENDIP  G
010  ANDREW         BUSH         HAR  MENDIP  B
001  JAMIE          CROSS        BARN DUNDRY  B
017  MICHAEL        EDGAR        HOB  MENDIP  B
027  DONALD         FORD         SKI  MENDIP  B
028       TANIA     FORD         SKI  MENDIP  G
011       CAROLINE  FOX          HAR  DUNDRY  G
002       KAREN     FRY          BARN DUNDRY  G
012  JEFFREY        GAMAN        HAR  DUNDRY  B
018       NICOLA    GRANGER      HOB  MENDIP  G
003  STEVEN         HARVEY       BARN MENDIP  B
004       TRACEY    HATHAWAY     BARN MENDIP  G
029       DEBORAH   HAWKES       SKI  DUNDRY  G
019       JULIE     HILL         HOB  DUNDRY  G
030  SHANE          HOBBS        SKI  DUNDRY  B
013       LISA      HOWARD       HAR  MENDIP  G
005  DAVID          HUGHES       BARN DUNDRY  B
014  ANDREW         LEWIS        HAR  MENDIP  B
020       TRACEY    MEACHAM      HOB  MENDIP  G
006       SHARON    MIZEN        BARN DUNDRY  G
015       JANE      NOTTON       HAR  DUNDRY  G
021       MANDY     OXENHAM      HOB  DUNDRY  G
031  NEIL           PAYNE        SKI  MENDIP  B
022  PAUL           RUSH         HOB  DUNDRY  B
016  DARREN         SUTTON       HAR  DUNDRY  B
023  KEITH          THOMPSON     HOB  MENDIP  B
007  GERRY          VOLLERO      BARN MENDIP  B
024  PAUL           WAGLAND      HOB  DUNDRY  B
032       LISA      WATKINS      SKI  MENDIP  G
008       TINA      WEST         BARN MENDIP  G

NUMBER OF BOYS  = 16
NUMBER OF GIRLS = 16
TOTAL           = 32
```

Figure 4.9
The Year Group now in alphabetical surname order.

```
YEAR FILE - TUTOR GROUP LIST FOR BARN

001  JAMIE          CROSS        BARN DUNDRY  B
002       KAREN     FRY          BARN DUNDRY  G
003  STEVEN         HARVEY       BARN MENDIP  B
004       TRACEY    HATHAWAY     BARN MENDIP  G
005  DAVID          HUGHES       BARN DUNDRY  B
006       SHARON    MIZEN        BARN DUNDRY  G
007  GERRY          VOLLERO      BARN MENDIP  B
008       TINA      WEST         BARN MENDIP  G

NUMBER OF BOYS  = 4
NUMBER OF GIRLS = 4
TOTAL           = 8


YEAR FILE - TUTOR GROUP LIST FOR HAR

009       LISA      BEDFORD      HAR  MENDIP  G
010  ANDREW         BUSH         HAR  MENDIP  B
011       CAROLINE  FOX          HAR  DUNDRY  G
012  JEFFREY        GAMAN        HAR  DUNDRY  B
013       LISA      HOWARD       HAR  MENDIP  G
014  ANDREW         LEWIS        HAR  MENDIP  B
015       JANE      NOTTON       HAR  DUNDRY  G
016  DARREN         SUTTON       HAR  DUNDRY  B

NUMBER OF BOYS  = 4
NUMBER OF GIRLS = 4
TOTAL           = 8


YEAR FILE - TUTOR GROUP LIST FOR HOB

017  MICHAEL        EDGAR        HOB  MENDIP  B
018       NICOLA    GRANGER      HOB  MENDIP  G
019       JULIE     HILL         HOB  DUNDRY  G
020       TRACEY    MEACHAM      HOB  MENDIP  G
021       MANDY     OXENHAM      HOB  DUNDRY  G
022  PAUL           RUSH         HOB  DUNDRY  B
023  KEITH          THOMPSON     HOB  MENDIP  B
024  PAUL           WAGLAND      HOB  DUNDRY  B

NUMBER OF BOYS  = 4
NUMBER OF GIRLS = 4
TOTAL           = 8


YEAR FILE - TUTOR GROUP LIST FOR SKI

025       KATHERINE BARNES       SKI  DUNDRY  G
026  DAVID          BARRINGTON   SKI  DUNDRY  B
027  DONALD         FORD         SKI  MENDIP  B
028       TANIA     FORD         SKI  MENDIP  G
029       DEBORAH   HAWKES       SKI  DUNDRY  G
030  SHANE          HOBBS        SKI  DUNDRY  B
031  NEIL           PAYNE        SKI  MENDIP  B
032       LISA      WATKINS      SKI  MENDIP  G

NUMBER OF BOYS  = 4
NUMBER OF GIRLS = 4
TOTAL           = 8
```

Figure 4.10
The Year Group now in their four Tutor Groups, still in alphabetical order.

Using a Database

```
YEAR FILE - HOUSE GROUP LIST FOR DUNDRY

025       KATHERINE  BARNES       SKI   DUNDRY  G
026  DAVID           BARRINGTON   SKI   DUNDRY  B
001  JAMIE           CROSS        BARN  DUNDRY  B
011       CAROLINE   FOX          HAR   DUNDRY  G
002       KAREN      FRY          BARN  DUNDRY  G
012  JEFFREY         GAMAN        HAR   DUNDRY  B
029       DEBORAH    HAWKES       SKI   DUNDRY  G
019       JULIE      HILL         HOB   DUNDRY  G
030  SHANE           HOBBS        SKI   DUNDRY  B
005  DAVID           HUGHES       BARN  DUNDRY  B
006       SHARON     MIZEN        BARN  DUNDRY  G
015       JANE       NOTTON       HAR   DUNDRY  G
021       MANDY      OXENHAM      HOB   DUNDRY  G
022  PAUL            RUSH         HOB   DUNDRY  B
016  DARREN          SUTTON       HAR   DUNDRY  B
024  PAUL            WAGLAND      HOB   DUNDRY  B

NUMBER OF BOYS  = 8
NUMBER OF GIRLS = 8
TOTAL           = 16

YEAR FILE - HOUSE GROUP LIST FOR MENDIP

009       LISA       BEDFORD      HAR   MENDIP  G
010  ANDREW          BUSH         HAR   MENDIP  B
017  MICHAEL         EDGAR        HOB   MENDIP  B
027  DONALD          FORD         SKI   MENDIP  B
028       TANIA      FORD         SKI   MENDIP  G
018       NICOLA     GRANGER      HOB   MENDIP  G
003  STEVEN          HARVEY       BARN  MENDIP  B
004       TRACEY     HATHAWAY     BARN  MENDIP  G
013       LISA       HOWARD       HAR   MENDIP  G
014  ANDREW          LEWIS        HAR   MENDIP  B
020       TRACEY     MEACHAM      HOB   MENDIP  G
031  NEIL            PAYNE        SKI   MENDIP  B
023  KEITH           THOMPSON     HOB   MENDIP  B
007  GERRY           VOLLERO      BARN  MENDIP  B
032       LISA       WATKINS      SKI   MENDIP  G
008       TINA       WEST         BARN  MENDIP  G

NUMBER OF BOYS  = 8
NUMBER OF GIRLS = 8
TOTAL           = 16
```

Figure 4.11
The Year Group now in their House groups.

```
YEAR FILE - BOYS

026  DAVID           BARRINGTON   SKI   DUNDRY  B
010  ANDREW          BUSH         HAR   MENDIP  B
001  JAMIE           CROSS        BARN  DUNDRY  B
017  MICHAEL         EDGAR        HOB   MENDIP  B
027  DONALD          FORD         SKI   MENDIP  B
012  JEFFREY         GAMAN        HAR   DUNDRY  B
003  STEVEN          HARVEY       BARN  MENDIP  B
030  SHANE           HOBBS        SKI   DUNDRY  B
005  DAVID           HUGHES       BARN  DUNDRY  B
014  ANDREW          LEWIS        HAR   MENDIP  B
031  NEIL            PAYNE        SKI   MENDIP  B
022  PAUL            RUSH         HOB   DUNDRY  B
016  DARREN          SUTTON       HAR   DUNDRY  B
023  KEITH           THOMPSON     HOB   MENDIP  B
007  GERRY           VOLLERO      BARN  MENDIP  B
024  PAUL            WAGLAND      HOB   DUNDRY  B

NUMBER OF BOYS = 16

YEAR FILE - GIRLS

025       KATHERINE  BARNES       SKI   DUNDRY  G
009       LISA       BEDFORD      HAR   MENDIP  G
028       TANIA      FORD         SKI   MENDIP  G
011       CAROLINE   FOX          HAR   DUNDRY  G
002       KAREN      FRY          BARN  DUNDRY  G
018       NICOLA     GRANGER      HOB   MENDIP  G
004       TRACEY     HATHAWAY     BARN  MENDIP  G
029       DEBORAH    HAWKES       SKI   DUNDRY  G
019       JULIE      HILL         HOB   DUNDRY  G
013       LISA       HOWARD       HAR   MENDIP  G
020       TRACEY     MEACHAM      HOB   MENDIP  G
006       SHARON     MIZEN        BARN  DUNDRY  G
015       JANE       NOTTON       HAR   DUNDRY  G
021       MANDY      OXENHAM      HOB   DUNDRY  G
032       LISA       WATKINS      SKI   MENDIP  G
008       TINA       WEST         BARN  MENDIP  G

NUMBER OF GIRLS = 16
```

Figure 4.12
The Boys and the Girls in the Year.

those teachers when selecting sports teams.

The final sort splits the boys from the girls and should be saved on disc as '1BOYS' and '1GIRLS'. (Figure 4.12) These single sex groups across the whole Year would be used at cross country time, for fitness testing or for P.E. reports if there was a different design for each gender.

The Year File disc, containing all these different files, would be available at any time to produce lists of pupils or to provide pupil data to help run other P.E. computer programs.

During each school year the Year File disc would need to be up-dated from time to time when new pupils entered the school or to change some individual pupil data. The Year File program will enable these operations to take place:

1. Add more pupil names.
2. Delete a whole pupil record – for pupils who leave school.
3. Change some of the data, for those occasions when a pupil changes Tutor Group, House or even surname. Spelling corrections to pupil names can also be made here.
4. Change Tutor Group or House names. At the end of the school Year these names may change and it is possible to change all pupil records from the old name to a new one.

At the end of the school year all the pupils would have to be 'moved' up a year. A new Year File would have to be created of pupils entering as first years. The moving up exercise might mean changing those Tutor Group or House names and changing the names of the data stored on disc from say YEAR4 to YEAR5. Year

```
! ALPHABETICAL YEAR LIST                                    !
!                                                           !
! 025 KATHERINE BARNES (SKI)   !      !      !      !        !
! 026 DAVID BARRINGTON (SKI)   !      !      !      !        !
! 009 LISA BEDFORD (HAR)       !      !      !      !        !
! 010 ANDREW BUSH (HAR)        !      !      !      !        !
! 001 JAMIE CROSS (BARN)       !      !      !      !        !
! 017 MICHAEL EDGAR (HOB)      !      !      !      !        !
! 027 DONALD FORD (SKI)        !      !      !      !        !
! 028 TANIA FORD (SKI)         !      !      !      !        !
! 011 CAROLINE FOX (HAR)       !      !      !      !        !
! 002 KAREN FRY (BARN)         !      !      !      !        !
! 012 JEFFREY GAMAN (HAR)      !      !      !      !        !
! 018 NICOLA GRANGER (HOB)     !      !      !      !        !
! 003 STEVEN HARVEY (BARN)     !      !      !      !        !
! 004 TRACEY HATHAWAY (BARN)   !      !      !      !        !
! 029 DEBORAH HAWKES (SKI)     !      !      !      !        !
! 019 JULIE HILL (HOB)         !      !      !      !        !
! 030 SHANE HOBBS (SKI)        !      !      !      !        !
! 013 LISA HOWARD (HAR)        !      !      !      !        !
! 005 DAVID HUGHES (BARN)      !      !      !      !        !
! 014 ANDREW LEWIS (HAR)       !      !      !      !        !
! 020 TRACEY MEACHAM (HOB)     !      !      !      !        !
! 006 SHARON MIZEN (BARN)      !      !      !      !        !
! 015 JANE NOTTON (HAR)        !      !      !      !        !
! 021 MANDY OXENHAM (HOB)      !      !      !      !        !
! 031 NEIL PAYNE (SKI)         !      !      !      !        !
! 022 PAUL RUSH (HOB)          !      !      !      !        !
! 016 DARREN SUTTON (HAR)      !      !      !      !        !
! 023 KEITH THOMPSON (HOB)     !      !      !      !        !
! 007 GERRY VOLLERO (BARN)     !      !      !      !        !
! 024 PAUL WAGLAND (HOB)       !      !      !      !        !
! 032 LISA WATKINS (SKI)       !      !      !      !        !
! 008 TINA WEST (BARN)         !      !      !      !        !
!                                                           !
! LIST PRINTED 26TH OCTOBER                                 !
```

Figure 4.13
A different way of presenting the Year Group.

records should be moved up from the top end of the school and not from the bottom end otherwise year data will be overwritten and lost.

YEAR5 deleted
YEAR4 is renamed YEAR5
YEAR3 is renamed YEAR4
YEAR2 is renamed YEAR3
YEAR1 is renamed YEAR2
The new YEAR1 file is then created.

Once familiar with the workings of a Year File program it does not take long to make the necessary changes each year. The bonus of the system is the way the data can be linked into other essential P.E. computer programs. The P.E. department may want to produce a list of all pupils, with lines and columns for recording different items. A short program will print these out, either as a whole year group (figure 4.13) or

```
! BOYS LIST - ALPHABETICAL                     !
!                                              !
! 026 DAVID BARRINGTON (SKI)  !    !    !    !  !
! 010 ANDREW BUSH (HAR)       !    !    !    !  !
! 001 JAMIE CROSS (BARN)      !    !    !    !  !
! 017 MICHAEL EDGAR (HOB)     !    !    !    !  !
! 027 DONALD FORD (SKI)       !    !    !    !  !
! 012 JEFFREY GAMAN (HAR)     !    !    !    !  !
! 003 STEVEN HARVEY (BARN)    !    !    !    !  !
! 030 SHANE HOBBS (SKI)       !    !    !    !  !
! 005 DAVID HUGHES (BARN)     !    !    !    !  !
! 014 ANDREW LEWIS (HAR)      !    !    !    !  !
! 031 NEIL PAYNE (SKI)        !    !    !    !  !
! 022 PAUL RUSH (HOB)         !    !    !    !  !
! 016 DARREN SUTTON (HAR)     !    !    !    !  !
! 023 KEITH THOMPSON (HOB)    !    !    !    !  !
! 007 GERRY VOLLERO (BARN)    !    !    !    !  !
! 024 PAUL WAGLAND (HOB)      !    !    !    !  !
!                                              !
! LIST PRINTED 26TH OCTOBER                    !
```

```
! GIRLS LIST - ALPHABETICAL                    !
!                                              !
! 025 KATHERINE BARNES (SKI)  !    !    !    !  !
! 009 LISA BEDFORD (HAR)      !    !    !    !  !
! 028 TANIA FORD (SKI)        !    !    !    !  !
! 011 CAROLINE FOX (HAR)      !    !    !    !  !
! 002 KAREN FRY (BARN)        !    !    !    !  !
! 018 NICOLA GRANGER (HOB)    !    !    !    !  !
! 004 TRACEY HATHAWAY (BARN)  !    !    !    !  !
! 029 DEBORAH HAWKES (SKI)    !    !    !    !  !
! 019 JULIE HILL (HOB)        !    !    !    !  !
! 013 LISA HOWARD (HAR)       !    !    !    !  !
! 020 TRACEY MEACHAM (HOB)    !    !    !    !  !
! 006 SHARON MIZEN (BARN)     !    !    !    !  !
! 015 JANE NOTTON (HAR)       !    !    !    !  !
! 021 MANDY OXENHAM (HOB)     !    !    !    !  !
! 032 LISA WATKINS (SKI)      !    !    !    !  !
! 008 TINA WEST (BARN)        !    !    !    !  !
!                                              !
! LIST PRINTED 26TH OCTOBER                    !
```

Figure 4.14
P.E. staff would use these kind of lists for many purposes throughout the year.

as separate boys/girls groups (figure 4.14) having obtained the names from the appropriate file held on disc. To do this manually for each year in the school would take a long time, to do this on the computer takes only a few minutes. No names have to be written out and being printed, it is neat, clear and easy to read.

Other uses of a database are examined in more detail in later chapters. A database can be a powerful tool for storing and analysing Sports Day records or entries. (see Chapter 7).

There are some database programs which will allow numerical data to be analysed statistically. There are situations where a P.E. teacher would like to carry out some analysis of say pupil performances but is put off by the complex mathematical calculations. (Chapter 8 examines how to carry out an analysis of fitness test figures.)

There will be some P.E. teachers who act as a

Using a Database

secretary of a school sports association where contact with many other schools will involve circulating and addressing many letters. Some database programs will allow names and addresses to be printed onto address labels so saving the teacher a great deal of time over the year.

Another use of a database program is for storing information about the stock held in the P.E. department although it may be preferred to hold this data in a spread sheet program (see Chapter 6 on stock control).

Much larger databases exist which can be accessed through a telephone connection (called a modem) to our computer. Through such a system we can even contact huge American databases and receive information on a wide variety of Physical Education issues.

British Telecom run a service called Prestel, a paged information database service like Oracle or Ceefax, which contains many thousands of pages, including many sections on sport. The Times Network, a schools database system, also has a sports section. These services cost money to join, in addition to the cost of the telephone call.

Options in Physical Education:

Many schools will operate some form of option scheme as part of their physical education programme for senior pupils. These pupils would normally be asked to fill in forms to select one or more activities out of those being offered. The P.E. teacher then has to analyse and publish the list of names for each activity.

In essence a simple task but a time consuming one. It can result in the teacher crawling around a paper strewn floor searching for particular choices before starting the mammoth task of writing out all the lists.

A computer will reduce considerably the amount of time it takes to analyse and print out the findings, especially if use was made of the pupil data from the Year File system already mentioned earlier in Chapter 4.

In planning an options programme there are five stages to cover before the scheme can operate. They are:

1. Decision making – which activities?
2. Preparation of option forms.
3. Filling in of forms by pupils.
4. Analysis of the choices.
5. Publication of lists.

To illustrate the effectiveness of such a computer program each of these stages will be followed using a small group of pupils as an example.

1. Decision making

Several decisions have to be made on the format of the option. The first will be related to the number of periods of time. In this example pupils are to be given a choice of activities in each of two periods of time, the First Half of term and the other in the Second Half of term.

Then there are decisions about the number of activities which are to be offered. These have to be realistic in terms of facilities, both inside and outside of school, and the availability of equipment. This analysis will offer the pupils four activities, namely Badminton, Volleyball, Table Tennis and Basketball. The number of activities a school offers might be greater than the number it can staff. This will initially give the pupils a wider choice. Once the pupils have made their choices and the numerical analysis has been completed further decisions on which of the options are viable then have to be made.

It can never be guaranteed that every pupil will be given their first choice. If only four wish to play basketball it cannot realistically run. One way of getting as much information from the pupils as possible at the time of filling in the option sheet is to ask them to make more than one choice. If pupils are asked to select three activities in order of preference for each period of time then the majority should be able to have their first choice but some may have to be given their second or even third choice. This system has to be carefully explained to pupils before the option takes place.

A computer program dealing with options should be able to handle whatever number of activities the P.E. staff wish to offer. This is arranged when setting up the program by indicating the number of activities and then inserting their names. These activities will now appear by name on the pupil questionnaire and in the subsequent analysis program.

Options in Physical Education

```
025   KATHERINE BARNES of SKI

P.E. COURSE CHOICES

This OPTION is for two periods of time .....
          ONE - FIRST HALF TERM
          TWO - SECOND HALF TERM
You are asked to choose which activity you would most like to do for EACH
period of time. In each column you should show this by writing 1, 2 and 3 next
to your three activities in your order of priority. Where possible you will be
given your first choice but sometimes your 2nd or 3rd choices may have to be
used.

ACTIVITY              ! ONE ! TWO !
01 BADMINTON          !     !     !
02 VOLLEYBALL         !     !     !
03 TABLE TENNIS       !     !     !
04 BASKETBALL         !     !     !
```

Figure 5.1
P.E. Option Form.

2. Preparation of option forms.

It is best to commit pupils to paper when they make their decisions about the activities they would most like to do. A general form could be produced which had space for pupils to fill in their own name as well as their choice of activity. How much better if each pupil received their own personalised form. Certain essential details must appear on any option form filled in by pupils. The pupils' name, their reference number and tutor group can all be taken from the Year File and printed out as part of the pre-arranged options form. The bonus for the teacher will be the ease with which the named form can be read and also that it will show the vital pupil reference number which will be used when inputting data at a later stage. (Figure 5.1)

An explanation of the selection procedure is essential on this option form particularly for those pupils who may be absent when they are first given out with the verbal explanation.

Once the computer has been primed with all the pupil and activity details, then the individual forms can be printed out.

3. Filling in of forms by pupils.

Pupils will have to fill in the absolute minimum once they have received their own form and so the operation takes only a few minutes. A brief verbal explanation may be needed to reinforce what is already explained on the form before the pupils put their 1, 2 and 3 in each column against the activities of their choice.

On that first occasion the teacher will be left with the named sheets of those who are absent. These pupils will need to be seen in a future lesson to complete their choices. The teacher will not have to spend a great deal of time in subsequent lessons explaining to these late pupils about the procedure of choice because of the full details contained in that form. Careful, advanced planning like this can always save time later on.

4. Anaylysis of the forms.

It is unlikely that all forms will be filled in on the first day. A computer program should be able to accept data on more than one occasion. It is also helpful to be able to insert the details of the pupils' choices in random order and not necessarily in reference number order or in alphabetical order as occurs in one of the cross country programs later (Chapter 9).

First the pupil is identified by their reference number on the form. Then the two sets of choices are entered. The named activities have also been given reference numbers so the user only has to enter into the computer the three activity numbers in order of priority for each of the two periods.

The seven numbers to be entered for each pupil only takes a few seconds to complete. Very quickly the majority of the group can be entered and their data saved and stored on disc. The remainder can be added later when they become available. A numerical analysis can be carried out at any time to see the trends.

The program will perform a number of operations on the data to help the teacher in selecting the list of activities which will operate and who will be in each group.

The first information the teacher wants from the computer is a numerical analysis for each activity, for each time period and for each of the three choices, in other words how many pupils want to do each activity. The teacher has to assess the first run through of this analysis

```
P.E. COURSE CHOICES

FIRST HALF TERM

                     FIRST CHOICE      SECOND CHOICE     THIRD CHOICE
                  BOYS GIRLS TOTAL   BOYS GIRLS TOTAL  BOYS GIRLS TOTAL

01 BADMINTON         4    4    8      4    3    7       6    6    12
02 VOLLEYBALL        4    8    12     6    3    9       3    2    5
03 TABLE TENNIS      4    3    7      3    6    9       3    3    6
04 BASKETBALL        3    1    4      2    4    6       3    5    8

P.E. COURSE CHOICES

SECOND HALF TERM

                     FIRST CHOICE      SECOND CHOICE     THIRD CHOICE
                  BOYS GIRLS TOTAL   BOYS GIRLS TOTAL  BOYS GIRLS TOTAL

01 BADMINTON         3    2    5      2    7    9       3    3    6
02 VOLLEYBALL        4    8    12     6    2    8       3    4    7
03 TABLE TENNIS      3    1    4      6    5    11      5    5    10
04 BASKETBALL        5    5    10     1    2    3       4    4    8
```

Figure 5.2
First Numerical Analysis of the P.E. Options. Basketball is not viable in the first Half Term.

(figure 5.2) and start to make decisions as to which activities are viable and which ones may not operate unless some changes are made.

Some pupils will have to be given their second or third choice and their data will have to be altered accordingly. The process is really no different from moving pieces of paper about from one pile to another. The difference is that much more data is available and it can be handled far more quickly.

Looking at the first choices for each period the only problem appears to be basketball in the first half term. Four pupils, in this case three boys and one girl is not a viable number whereas the remainder can play their particular game.

The computer can produce a list of all the

pupils with their choices which will prove useful when having to move pupils into other activities.

```
PUPIL DATA FOR P.E. COURSE CHOICES
025  KATHERINE BARNES ------ 03 01 02 ** 01 04 02
026  DAVID BARRINGTON ------ 03 02 01 ** 02 04 03
009  LISA BEDFORD ---------- 02 04 01 ** 04 02 01
010  ANDREW BUSH ----------- 01 02 04 ** 04 03 02
001  JAMIE CROSS ----------- 02 01 03 ** 04 01 02
017  MICHAEL EDGAR --------- 04 03 02 ** 03 02 01
027  DONALD FORD ----------- 01 02 03 ** 01 02 03
028  TANIA FORD ------------ 04 03 01 ** 02 03 04
011  CAROLINE FOX ---------- 02 03 04 ** 02 01 03
002  KAREN FRY ------------- 01 04 02 ** 02 03 01
012  JEFFREY GAMAN --------- 03 04 01 ** 04 03 01
018  NICOLA GRANGER -------- 02 03 01 ** 02 03 01
003  STEVEN HARVEY --------- 02 04 01 ** 02 03 04
004  TRACEY HATHAWAY ------- 01 03 04 ** 04 01 03
029  DEBORAH HAWKES -------- 01 02 03 ** 02 04 03
019  JULIE HILL ------------ 02 03 01 ** 04 03 02
030  SHANE HOBBS ----------- 01 02 04 ** 02 03 04
013  LISA HOWARD ----------- 02 01 03 ** 04 01 03
005  DAVID HUGHES ---------- 01 02 03 ** 04 03 02
014  ANDREW LEWIS ---------- 02 03 01 ** 03 02 01
020  TRACEY MEACHAM -------- 03 02 04 ** 01 02 04
006  SHARON MIZEN ---------- 02 04 01 ** 03 01 02
015  JANE NOTTON ----------- 01 04 03 ** 04 01 02
021  MANDY OXENHAM --------- 02 01 04 ** 02 03 04
031  NEIL PAYNE ------------ 00 00 00 ** 00 00 00
022  PAUL RUSH ------------- 03 01 02 ** 03 02 04
016  DARREN SUTTON --------- 03 01 02 ** 04 02 03
023  KEITH THOMPSON -------- 04 03 01 ** 04 01 02
007  GERRY VOLLERO --------- 02 01 04 ** 01 02 03
024  PAUL WAGLAND ---------- 04 02 01 ** 01 03 04
032  LISA WATKINS ---------- 03 02 04 ** 02 01 03
008  TINA WEST ------------- 02 03 01 ** 02 01 04
```

Figure 5.3
Summary of choices made by pupils.

Figure 5.3 shows the whole group with their reference numbers, the three numbers before the stars are the three choices for the first half term followed by the other three choices after the stars.

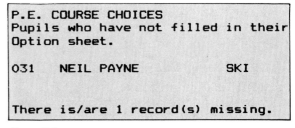

```
P.E. COURSE CHOICES
Pupils who have not filled in their
Option sheet.

031    NEIL PAYNE              SKI


There is/are 1 record(s) missing.
```

Figure 5.4
The program will print out the missing records.

Anyone registering a full set of zeros will not have made their choice. These absentees can be printed out by asking the computer to publish the full list of missing records (figure 5.4), in this

Options in Physical Education

case there is only one pupil. There is no point producing 'final' lists if there are still many pupil choices outstanding. In this analysis one missing pupil will not significantly affect the final outcome as to which activity runs so the final decision may be made without his choice.

```
P.E. COURSE CHOICES
FIRST HALF TERM

BASKETBALL   FIRST CHOICE

017   MICHAEL EDGAR          HOB
028       TANIA FORD         SKI
023   KEITH THOMPSON         HOB
024   PAUL WAGLAND           HOB


Number of BOYS  = 3
Number of GIRLS = 1
Total Number    = 4
```

Figure 5.5
Who chose Basketball? Their choices must be changed now that it will not run.

Those four basketball players have to be identified (figure 5.5) before they can be moved. By referring back to figure 5.3 the second choices of these pupils have to be assertained. They are:

Michael Edgar – Table Tennis
Tania Ford – Table Tennis
Keith Thompson – Table Tennis
Paul Wagland – Volleyball

To add these four to those pupils who had already chosen those activities presents no practical teaching problems and so their data can be changed. Once their data has been changed it is wise to run another numerical analysis to obtain a final check, figure 5.6. It will also be necessary to print out a final list of all the pupil data, figure 5.7, which now shows those four with their new activites appearing as first choices.

5. Publication of lists.

A list of the final pupil choices can be produced as soon as the decisions have been made on which activities will or will not run and

```
P.E. COURSE CHOICES

FIRST HALF TERM

                    FIRST CHOICE
                    BOYS GIRLS TOTAL

01 BADMINTON         5     4     9
02 VOLLEYBALL        4     8     12
03 TABLE TENNIS      7     4     11
04 BASKETBALL        0     0     0


P.E. COURSE CHOICES

SECOND HALF TERM

                    FIRST CHOICE
                    BOYS GIRLS TOTAL

01 BADMINTON         4     2     6
02 VOLLEYBALL        4     8     12
03 TABLE TENNIS      3     1     4
04 BASKETBALL        5     5     10
```

Figure 5.6
Now the changes are completed the final numerical analysis.

```
PUPIL DATA FOR P.E. COURSE CHOICES
025   KATHERINE BARNES --------- 03 01 02 ** 01 04 02
026   DAVID BARRINGTON --------- 03 02 01 ** 02 04 03
009   LISA BEDFORD ------------- 02 04 01 ** 04 02 01
010   ANDREW BUSH -------------- 01 02 04 ** 04 03 02
001   JAMIE CROSS -------------- 02 01 03 ** 04 01 02
017   MICHAEL EDGAR ------------ 03 02 04 ** 03 02 01
027   DONALD FORD -------------- 01 02 03 ** 01 02 03
028   TANIA FORD --------------- 03 01 04 ** 02 03 04
011   CAROLINE FOX ------------- 02 03 04 ** 02 01 03
002   KAREN FRY ---------------- 01 04 02 ** 02 03 01
012   JEFFREY GAMAN ------------ 03 04 01 ** 04 03 01
018   NICOLA GRANGER ----------- 02 03 01 ** 02 03 01
003   STEVEN HARVEY ------------ 02 04 01 ** 02 03 04
004   TRACEY HATHAWAY ---------- 01 03 04 ** 04 01 03
029   DEBORAH HAWKES ----------- 01 02 03 ** 02 04 03
019   JULIE HILL --------------- 02 03 01 ** 04 03 02
030   SHANE HOBBS -------------- 01 02 04 ** 02 03 04
013   LISA HOWARD -------------- 02 01 03 ** 04 01 03
005   DAVID HUGHES ------------- 01 02 03 ** 04 03 02
014   ANDREW LEWIS ------------- 02 03 01 ** 03 02 01
020   TRACEY MEACHAM ----------- 03 02 04 ** 01 02 04
006   SHARON MIZEN ------------- 02 04 01 ** 03 01 02
015   JANE NOTTON -------------- 01 04 03 ** 04 01 02
021   MANDY OXENHAM ------------ 02 01 04 ** 02 03 04
031   NEIL PAYNE --------------- 03 02 01 ** 01 02 03
022   PAUL RUSH ---------------- 03 01 02 ** 03 02 04
016   DARREN SUTTON ------------ 03 01 02 ** 04 02 03
023   KEITH THOMPSON ----------- 03 01 04 ** 02 01 03
007   GERRY VOLLERO ------------ 02 01 04 ** 01 02 03
024   PAUL WAGLAND ------------- 01 04 02 ** 01 03 04
032   LISA WATKINS ------------- 03 02 04 ** 02 01 03
008   TINA WEST ---------------- 02 03 01 ** 02 01 04
```

Figure 5.7
The final list of pupil data.

once the necessary changes have been made to the pupil data. (Figure 5.8) This is the list which would go up on the notice board for pupils to see. It shows the activities which they will be taking, by name, for each of the two periods.

The other lists which will be required are those showing which pupils are taking each activity. In effect these are the teachers' lists to register those present each week. Figure 5.9 shows the volleyball group for the first half term and table tennis for the second half term, but there will be a separate list for all the other viable activities.

At no time during this operation has anyone written out any names of pupils or activities. The teachers' lists and those for the pupils are all of a high quality being produced by the computer printer. P.E. staff and pupils will be able to obtain the results of this options analysis far quicker by using the computer than if it had been analysed by hand and the office staff had to type out the lists from a hand written draft. A further advantage of using the computer is that lists can be easily up-dated and re-printed should there be any unforseen changes.

The advantage of using the computer for this type of analysis is not only because it saves a great deal of time but also because it adds significantly to the quality of the presentation of the whole of the options scheme.

```
P.E.  COURSE CHOICES
FIRST HALF TERM

VOLLEYBALL   FIRST CHOICE

009      LISA BEDFORD           HAR
001   JAMIE CROSS               BARN
011      CAROLINE FOX           HAR
018      NICOLA GRANGER         HOB
003   STEVEN HARVEY             BARN
019      JULIE HILL             HOB
013      LISA HOWARD            HAR
014   ANDREW LEWIS              HAR
006      SHARON MIZEN           BARN
021      MANDY OXENHAM          HOB
007   GERRY VOLLERO             BARN
008      TINA WEST              BARN


Number of BOYS  = 4
Number of GIRLS = 8
Total Number    = 12

P.E.  COURSE CHOICES
SECOND HALF TERM

TABLE TENNIS   FIRST CHOICE

017   MICHAEL EDGAR             HOB
014   ANDREW LEWIS              HAR
006      SHARON MIZEN           BARN
022   PAUL RUSH                 HOB


Number of BOYS  = 3
Number of GIRLS = 1
Total Number    = 4
```

Figure 5.9
The final print-out shows all the pupils who will be taking part in each activity.

```
P.E.  COURSE CHOICES

                              FIRST HALF TERM  SECOND HALF TERM
025   KATHERINE BARNES    SKI   TABLE TENNIS   BADMINTON
026   DAVID BARRINGTON    SKI   TABLE TENNIS   VOLLEYBALL
009   LISA BEDFORD        HAR   VOLLEYBALL     BASKETBALL
010   ANDREW BUSH         HAR   BADMINTON      BASKETBALL
001   JAMIE CROSS         BARN  VOLLEYBALL     BASKETBALL
017   MICHAEL EDGAR       HOB   TABLE TENNIS   TABLE TENNIS
027   DONALD FORD         SKI   BADMINTON      BADMINTON
028   TANIA FORD          SKI   TABLE TENNIS   VOLLEYBALL
011   CAROLINE FOX        HAR   VOLLEYBALL     VOLLEYBALL
002   KAREN FRY           BARN  BADMINTON      VOLLEYBALL
012   JEFFREY GAMAN       HAR   TABLE TENNIS   BASKETBALL
018   NICOLA GRANGER      HOB   VOLLEYBALL     VOLLEYBALL
003   STEVEN HARVEY       BARN  VOLLEYBALL     VOLLEYBALL
004   TRACEY HATHAWAY     BARN  BADMINTON      BASKETBALL
029   DEBORAH HAWKES      SKI   BADMINTON      VOLLEYBALL
019   JULIE HILL          HOB   VOLLEYBALL     BASKETBALL
030   SHANE HOBBS         SKI   BADMINTON      VOLLEYBALL
013   LISA HOWARD         HAR   VOLLEYBALL     BASKETBALL
005   DAVID HUGHES        BARN  BADMINTON      BASKETBALL
014   ANDREW LEWIS        HAR   VOLLEYBALL     TABLE TENNIS
020   TRACEY MEACHAM      HOB   TABLE TENNIS   BADMINTON
006   SHARON MIZEN        BARN  VOLLEYBALL     TABLE TENNIS
015   JANE NOTTON         HAR   BADMINTON      BASKETBALL
021   MANDY OXENHAM       HOB   VOLLEYBALL     VOLLEYBALL
031   NEIL PAYNE          SKI   TABLE TENNIS   BADMINTON
022   PAUL RUSH           HOB   TABLE TENNIS   TABLE TENNIS
016   DARREN SUTTON       HAR   TABLE TENNIS   BASKETBALL
023   KEITH THOMPSON      HOB   TABLE TENNIS   VOLLEYBALL
007   GERRY VOLLERO       BARN  VOLLEYBALL     BADMINTON
024   PAUL WAGLAND        HOB   BADMINTON      BADMINTON
032   LISA WATKINS        SKI   TABLE TENNIS   VOLLEYBALL
008   TINA WEST           BARN  VOLLEYBALL     VOLLEYBALL
```

Figure 5.8
The list of allocated activities for the P.E. notice board.

Options in Physical Education

Stock Control and Financial Accountability

Every Physical Education department has to be accountable for the stock of equipment which it holds. The number of hockey sticks or tennis balls which we have in our store rooms have traditionally been recorded in a book which the auditors check during their annual inspection.

Some schools may have to be more accountable than others if they do not have a school Bursar to look after the accounts. In this case not only do numbers of items have to be recorded but also costs and totals.

There are two ways that a computer can be used to assist in the handling of these figures. One possibility is to use a DATABASE program whilst the other way would involve a SPREAD SHEET. The latter may be thought of as a program with applications more appropriate for the business world. P.E. teachers may not need to carry out the same complex financial analysis as in industry or commerce but these computer programs will save a great deal of time when recording and calculating their figures.

THE DATABASE

Some database programs have a capacity to calculate numerical data, but not all database programs have that option, so beware. In the main, stock control within a P.E. department is concerned mainly with the recording of each and every item of equipment, large and small, which is held in the department.

Equipment may be distributed over a wide area and held in different store rooms, cupboards, offices, gymnasia, sports halls or even different buildings. Using a normal database program we can set up a system of recording which can be extremely helpful to us when it comes to stock taking as well as being an efficient recording medium.

To set up such a system seven details for each item of equipment should be entered into the database.
1. ACTIVITY
2. ITEM
3. WHERE
4. YEAR 1 (being used)
5. YEAR 1 (in stock or bought new)
6. YEAR 2 (being used)
7. YEAR 2 (in stock or bought new)

We need to identify each piece of equipment with an 'activity' as well as give a description of each 'item'. This description should be quite specific indicating where appropriate their weights or types. This is particularly helpful for recording the separate sizes of equipment such as javelins or tape measures, etc. When equipment is stored in several places it is useful to identify 'where' each piece is kept.

When looking at the needs to record the actual figures it is only really necessary to hold two years of figures at a time. It is also better to separate those items which are currently being used during day to day teaching as distinct from

Stock Control

those items which are currently held in stock and are brand new or items which are purchased during the course of the year.

When stock taking is carried out it is useful to be able to check the amount of equipment which was held for each item during the previous year. Adjustments can be made to totals at the end of the financial year before retaining on disc the previous year and the setting up of the new list for the following year.

As each entry has three parts to its description it means that all items can be quickly sorted and displayed according to their activity, their name or their location. To carry out such a sort using normal book-keeping techniques would usually involve the checking of several pages and then writing a new list on a piece of paper. Once the descriptions and figures are in the computer, sorting can be quickly carried out under the different headings and sent to the printer. These print outs can then be used to help with stock taking or even given to the auditor.

Initially items can be entered in any order and then re-sorted afterwards. If at any time information is required on all athletics equipment held by the department the computer can be requested to print out all those records whose activity is identical to 'athletics'. (Figure 6.1)

```
STOCK CONTROL - ATHLETICS EQUIPMENT
-----------------------------------

ACTIVITY   ITEM            WHERE   1985  NEW85 1986  NEW86
-----------------------------------------------------------
ATHLETICS DISCUS 1.00      STORE   28    6     30    4
ATHLETICS DISCUS 1.25      STORE   8     2     8     2
ATHLETICS DISCUS 1.50      STORE   4     0     4     0
ATHLETICS DISCUS 2.00      STORE   1     0     1     0
ATHLETICS HJ LATHE         GYM     4     1     3     1
ATHLETICS HJ STANDS        GYM     1 PR  0     1 PR  0
ATHLETICS JAVELIN 600GM    STORE   20    6     20    4
ATHLETICS JAVELIN 700GM    STORE   10    2     10    2
ATHLETICS JAVELIN 800GM    STORE   2     0     2     0
ATHLETICS RAKE             STORE   2     0     2     0
ATHLETICS RELAY BATON      OFFICE  12    4     12    4
ATHLETICS SHOT 3.25        STORE   15    0     14    0
ATHLETICS SHOT 4.00        STORE   6     0     6     0
ATHLETICS SHOT 5.00        STORE   4     0     4     0
ATHLETICS TAPE 20 METRES   OFFICE  2     0     3     1
ATHLETICS TAPE 30 METRES   OFFICE  2     0     1     0
ATHLETICS TAPE 60 METRES   OFFICE  0     0     2     0
```

Figure 6.1
Stock Control using a database.

Similarly, if we wanted to extract only the details of all our discus equipment then the database could be asked to print out those records whose 'ITEM' contained the word 'DISCUS'.

The advantage of this database system over a spread sheet is this type of sorting and selective searching for data. Using a sort on the 'WHERE' category and asking for all items which are located in the 'STORE' we can then print out such a list and take it to that storeroom for a quick and easy check of the quantity of each item kept there. Book-keeping methods of stock taking involve a great deal of time turning over pages to locate items which always seem to be listed in the wrong order.

The number of recorded items for each piece of equipment can be altered on the paper copy and later such alterations transferred to the computer. An up-to-date print out can then be produced without any of the normal crossing out or alterations usually associated with the book-keeping method. The quality of these print outs means that they can be readily understood by all who use, see or check them.

For those databases which can be programmed to make calculations then further columns or rows can be allocated for adding up the totals.

THE SPREAD SHEET

A spread sheet is primarily used for rapid calculations of many figures which would otherwise take a long time to work out on paper. The spread sheet is particularly useful when the cost of each item of P.E. equipment has to be recorded. The spread sheet can be programmed to calculate the total value of the stock or make predictions of the total costs of our future requirements. Once the figures are entered these calculations take only seconds, but there has to be some careful planning and preparations before that is possible. Certain 'formulae' have to be entered, such as multiplying 'quantity' by 'cost' to give the 'total' value or adding up all figures in a row to provide another total.

To set up the spread sheet the various catagories or headings have to be decided upon. As spread sheets deal principally with numerical data, we may not be able to indicate as much written information, such as the associated 'activity' or 'where' each item is stored, as we did with the database. It will be possible to write in a description of each 'item' but in a slightly

	ITEM	VALUE	STOCK	TOTAL	REQUIRE	COST
DISCUS	1.00 KG	870	30	26100	4	3480
DISCUS	1.25 KG	920	8	7360	2	1840
DISCUS	1.50 KG	1085	4	4340	0	0
DISCUS	2.00 KG	1225	1	1225	0	0
H.J.	LATHE	880	3	2640	1	880
H.J.	STAND	2900	1	2900	0	0
JAVELIN	600 GM	2450	20	49000	4	9800
JAVELIN	700 GM	2590	10	25900	2	5180
JAVELIN	800 GM	2890	2	5780	0	0
RAKE		500	2	1000	0	0
RELAY	BATONS	133	12	1596	4	532
SHOT	3.25 KG	590	14	8260	0	0
SHOT	4.00 KG	700	6	4200	0	0
SHOT	5.00 KG	840	4	3360	0	0
TAPE	20 M	1290	3	3870	1	1290
TAPE	30 M	1590	1	1590	0	0
TAPE	60 M	2190	2	4380	0	0
TOTALS			123	153501	18	23002

Figure 6.2
Stock Control using a spread sheet.

different way.

In the example shown in figure 6.2 information related to athletics equipment for the period of a single year is displayed. The catagories here are
  1. ITEM of equipment
  2. VALUE of each item in pence
  3. The number of items in STOCK
  4. The TOTAL value of this stock
  5. The number of new items we REQUIRE for the following year
  6. The COST of buying these new items.

Having created these headings for each of the columns, details of every item is entered down the rows. Once these have been entered a further space at the bottom can be allocated for the calculation of the column TOTALS. Once this structure has been drafted, and it is usually best to plan this on graph paper beforehand, then the formulae can be entered for our calculations.

Three pieces of information are supplied by the teacher – the 'value', the number in 'stock' and the items we 'require'. In the example, six calculations are being made by the computer to fill in the grid. By entering a formulae in each row, the computer can calculate the TOTAL value of each item of stock. This is done by multiplying our VALUE figure with the STOCK number. Similarly, by multiplying VALUE and REQUIRE, the computer calculates the COST of the new equipment.

Most spread sheet programs have a simple way of inserting such formulae into each row down the whole column avoiding repetition.

At the bottom of each of the four columns,

opposite the word TOTALS, we can make the computer add up the whole of each column. Once the computer is asked to evaluate the model we can see that we have 123 items of athletics equipment which have a value of £1,535-01 and the cost of purchasing the 18 items we require would be £230-02.

This information can be shown on the screen or like the database printed out on paper. Spread sheets may have many columns, too many to be printed out in one operation, but parts can be selected and joined together once printed on paper. On the screen a spread sheet can be scrolled (moved) up or down or from side to side to see any part of the whole sheet. It is possible with some databases or with some spread sheets that they can be linked up to a graphics program which will convert the numerical data into a graphic form. The spread sheet can be programmed to obtain separate totals for the value of equipment held in the P.E. department for each of the different activity catagories. The total value for equipment for athletics, badminton, hockey, etc., might look like this:

ACTIVITY	TOTAL (£'s)
Athletics	1535
Badminton	421
Basketball	342
Cricket	1492
Football	882
Hockey	746
Netball	483
Rounders	321
Rugby	592
Softball	98
Swimming	283
Volleyball	461

This information could then be displayed in different ways through the graphics program. Figures 6.3, 6.4, 6.5 and 6.6 show these activity figures displayed as a line graph a bar chart or a pie chart, ordinary and emphasised. The computer program may make certain decisions for itself when composing these graphs or charts. In the case of the pie charts the amount for Softball was determined to be so small in

Stock Control

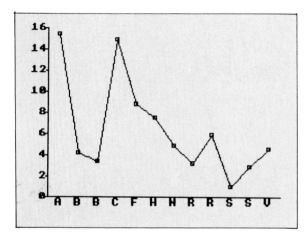

Figure 6.3
Cost of equipment displayed as a Line Graph.

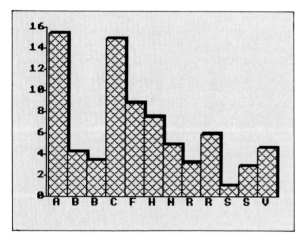

Figure 6.4
Cost of equipment displayed as a Bar Chart.

department with a visual image of the relative amounts of money invested in the different activities. We all know that it is more expensive to purchase equipment for some activities that it is for others but do we always know by how much?. It would be a very low priority, in terms of time, to produce these types of graphs by hand but by using the computer they can be produced and printed out within minutes and provide information not previously available to the department.

There are bank account management

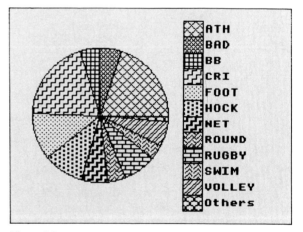

Figure 6.5
Cost of equipment displayed as a Pie Chart.

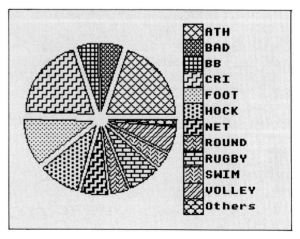

Figure 6.6
Cost of equipment displayed as an Emphasised Pie Chart.

comparison to the rest that the computer decided to classify it as 'others' instead of 'softball'.

This particular graphics program takes the first letter of each activity to label the columns and so you would have to insert an explanation of this to understand that A stands for athletics, the first B for Badminton and the second B for Basketball, and so on.

This form of analysis may not be considered as an essential element of departmental administration. It does, however, provide the programs which would handle and analyse all transactions in a school sports fund or school trip account. They will record all income and expenditure, allow you to search, amend or delete information as well as produce an up to date balance of the account. Like the spread sheet program details from the bank account can be displayed in graphics form. Such a program could be of great assistance to anyone taking on the responsibility of the Treasurer of a school sports association.

How much use a P.E. department makes of these types of computer programs will depend on the accountability demands made by the school. They will save time, cut out errors and present a clear picture of the stock held in, or the financial position of the P.E. department.

Stock Control

Sports Day

Using computers is only worthwhile if they improve the quality of an event or they are more efficient than using traditional methods. Most schools organise an annual athletics sports day and there are many aspects of that organisation where using a computer should be seriously considered by the P.E. teacher. Equally the computer could be used to assist with the organisation and running of inter school, inter District or County Athletics competitions.

The areas where a computer could be used would be in connection with:

1. General information
2. Entries
3. Results analysis
4. School records
5. Results publication

1. GENERAL INFORMATION

Each year staff and pupils have to be informed and reminded of the format as well as the rules and regulations governing the running of the Sports Day or athletics event. Normally these regulations do not change significantly from year to year and therefore such information could be stored on disc having been typed out on the computer using a word processor. Each year the new version can be swiftly up-dated, normally this only involves changing the date, before being printed, photo-copied and circulated around all concerned.

The word processor can even be used to produce the printed recording sheets for use during the various athletic events. (Figure 7.1) The advantage of producing your own recording sheets is that some additional information can be inserted, such as the points scored for the track events. This may seem a minor point but it is better to have this standardised before the event than to have people inserting it on the day when mistakes might be made under pressure.

HARTCLIFFE SCHOOL
ATHLETICS SPORTS DAY
TRACK EVENT RESULT SHEET

EVENT NO.

EVENT   YEAR BOYS/GIRLS

POS	NAME	HOUSE	TIME	PTS
1st				10
2nd				8
3rd				6
4th				5
5th				4
6th				3
7th				2
8th				1

HARTCLIFFE SCHOOL
ATHLETICS SPORTS DAY
HIGH JUMP RESULT SHEET

EVENT NO.

EVENT   YEAR BOYS/GIRLS HIGH JUMP

NAME	HSE				BEST	POS	PTS

Sports Day

Figure 7.1
Examples of Sports Day recording sheets produced by the word processor.

2. ENTRIES

It depends how 'official' a P.E. teacher wants to make Sports Day in terms of receiving entries and recording names of all competitors before the day. It may be that competitors names will only be listed and kept by the 'team manager' and not by the event organiser. In this way competitors names would only be entered onto the event recording sheets by the event official during Sports Day.

If entries are required earlier then competitors names can be entered onto event recording sheets. The only problem with this method occurs when pupils who are absent or injured on the day have to be replaced by other names.

For those who like to have their entries beforehand, and this would certainly arise with say a County event, then computer programs can be of considerable help.

A database type program could be set up to handle the complexities of entries where competitors are only allowed to enter a certain number of track or field events. Take as an example a Sports Day event where pupils may enter two track and two field events. As boys and girls generally compete separately then two identical files could initially be set up, one for each gender. If the entry list is likely to be small then both boys and girls could be entered in one file. Eight 'fields' would be required to set up the database and these would be:

1. NAME
2. HOUSE (This could be school for an inter school event.)
3. YEAR
4. GENDER
5. TRACK1
6. TRACK2
7. FIELD1
8. FIELD2

More than eight fields could be entered depending on the type of event. Other extra information might include the competitors number or additional track or field events. The wordprocessor could be used to produce a standard entry form, figure 7.2.

Entries could then be typed into the computer in any order, a Year group at a time or even a House group at a time. Typing in the information would be carried out like this:

1. NAME   : GREEN JUNE
2. HOUSE   : MENDIP
3. YEAR   : 2 HAR
4. GENDER : G
5. TRACK 1 : 100M
6. TRACK 2 : 200M

Figure 7.2
Sports Day Entry Form.

7. FIELD 1 : LJ
8. FIELD 2 : HJ

In figure 7.3 twelve sports day entries have been received and entered into a database program. Because there are only a few entries boys and girls have been entered together. The computer can sort and print out this list in a variety of ways. Here the list is in alphabetical order in their House groups.

```
SPORTS DAY ENTRIES
------------------

NAME          HOUSE   YEAR   GENDER TRACK1  TRACK2  FIELD1  FIELD2
-----------------------------------------------------------------
BUSH ANN      DUNDRY  1SKI   G      100M    200M    SHOT
CLEMENT MARK  DUNDRY  2HAR   B      200M    400M    SHOT    JAVELIN
FORD LIZ      DUNDRY  2HOB   G      200M    800M    L.J.    JAVELIN
KNEE HELEN    DUNDRY  2HAR   G      100M    400M    L.J.
RED MIKE      DUNDRY  2HAR   B                      L.J.
SMITH SIMON   DUNDRY  1SKI   B      200M    100M    SHOT
WEEKS ALISON  DUNDRY  1SKI   G                      SHOT
WHITE IAN     DUNDRY  1SKI   B      100M    200M
BLACK EMMA    MENDIP  2HAR   G      800M            L.J.    JAVELIN
DAW TERRY     MENDIP  1BARN  B      100M    200M
GRAY JAN      MENDIP  1BARN  G      400M            SHOT    H.J.
GREEN JUNE    MENDIP  2HAR   G      100M    200M    L.J.    H.J.
HAND JIM      MENDIP  2HOB   B      100M    400M    L.J.    DISCUS
HAND LEE      MENDIP  1BARN  B      100M            L.J.
SUTTON SARAH  MENDIP  1BARN  G      100M            SHOT
YELLOW JOHN   MENDIP  2HOB   B                      SHOT    DISCUS
```

Figure 7.3
Various Sports Day Entries ready for sorting.

From this program we can also print out a list of competitors in every event. To obtain the names of all those competing in an event, such as the Year 1 Boys 100M, we will need to carry out the following procedure. First we need to find a way of extracting only those in the 100M. In some entries the 100M appears under TRACK1 whilst others have their 100M under TRACK2. A database ought to be able to perform a search given certain conditions. The conditions laid down for this search will be that we want to only 'Boys' in Year "1" and that we want to check whether TRACK1 or TRACK2 contains "100M". If these four conditions apply then we want those names printed out. (Figure 7.4) Similarly, a list can be printed for the Year 2 Girls Long Jump event. (Figure 7.5) The teacher would continue this process for all the other events. Suitable headings can be added so that the printed list is clearly labelled with the year group and event.

A comprehensive and detailed "official" Sports Day programme can be made up from these lists. The programme should also include an

```
SPORTS DAY ENTRIES
------------------

1ST YEAR BOYS 100M
------------------

NAME               HOUSE    YEAR
-----------------------------------

SMITH SIMON        DUNDRY   1SKI
WHITE  IAN         DUNDRY   1SKI
DAW TERRY          MENDIP   1BARN
HAND LEE           MENDIP   1BARN
```

Figure 7.4
Searching the database will locate all competitors in the 1st Year Boys 100m.

```
SPORTS DAY ENTRIES
------------------

2ND YEAR GIRLS LONG JUMP
------------------------

NAME               HOUSE    YEAR
-----------------------------------

FORD LIZ           DUNDRY   2HOB
KNEE HELEN         DUNDRY   2HAR
BLACK EMMA         MENDIP   2HAR
```

Figure 7.5
The girls competing in the Long Jump.

Figure 7.6
The order of events.

```
SPORTS DAY EVENTS

001   1ST YEAR    100M    GIRLS
002   1ST YEAR    100M    BOYS
003   2ND YEAR    100M    GIRLS
004   2ND YEAR    100M    BOYS
005   1ST YEAR    L.J.    GIRLS
006   1ST YEAR    L.J.    BOYS
007   2ND YEAR    L.J.    GIRLS
008   2ND YEAR    L.J.    BOYS
009   1ST YEAR    SHOT    GIRLS
010   1ST YEAR    SHOT    BOYS
011   2ND YEAR    SHOT    GIRLS
012   2ND YEAR    SHOT    BOYS
```

Sports Day

order of events (figure 7.6) which can be quickly written out using the wordprocessor. It may be necessary to use the cut and paste method and a photo-copier to produce this programme.

An alternative way of dealing with entries is to have a specially written computer program which would serve two purposes. Firstly it would deal with the entries in a similar way to the database. Secondly it would act as the means of providing competitors' data for the production of the results. This aspect will be examined later.

3. RESULTS ANALYSIS

There is nothing worse during the running of a school sports day, or athletics match, than to have finished all the events and then have to wait half an hour or more whilst the recorders have to work out the final result.

This sometimes occurs when too much is asked of the recorders. It can take a long time to write down onto a master recording sheet all the details from every track and field event recording sheet. This may involve writing down every competitors name and their performances as well as the team scores and running team totals. A large number of results sheets arriving towards the end of an athletics event will soon cause a delay in calculating the final result.

Even if the recorders are asked only to add up the team points and keep a running team total there can still be a delay at the end using a 'paper' system. This can occur if the master recording sheet has had all the events listed on the left with blank columns for results on the right. The problem occurs because results never arrive at the recorder in the order written on the sheet. When several event recording sheets arrive at the end there may be long columns of figures to add up before the final result is obtained.

If it is accepted that the priority for the recorders during the course of a school sports day event or athletics meeting is to have available an up to date score at any time then this can easily be achieved by using a suitable computer program instead of using the paper and pencil method. Details of individual performances do not need to be written out again from the event recording sheets during the sports day. These can be given to the announcer to broadcast as

the event goes on once the recorder has noted the team points. They can then be displayed outside the recording 'hut' or through a window for the athletes to see. It is most important that the announcer receives a regular up-date of the team scores with the final result being available within minutes of the last event finishing.

The computer program to be used for this purpose should deal only with the numerical analysis of the team scores. It will handle the details of the points scored by each team in the various events and it will store that information so that totals can be obtained at the press of a button.

Preparation well before Sports Day is essential as the computer program has to be set up with details of each event and then saved on disc. If the same events occur annually then the event data can be recalled from the disc used the previous year. The details that are required include the event number, the event itself and whether is is a boy's or a girl's event. The event number is used not only to identify the event recording sheet but it is also used when entering details of the team points into the computer.

During sports day, the computer should be placed near to or next to the announcer. No more than two recorders would be needed to operate the system, preferably one having some keyboard experience. The recorder at the computer, could be a teacher or even a pupil who was not competing, but they ought to be experienced at using a computer. When a result sheet arrives from a track or a field event one of the recorders should check or insert the individual points scored and then add up the team points. These team points are then fed into the computer by the computer operator and the result sheet can then be given straight to the announcer.

Only numbers are fed into the computer. First the event number which will bring confirmation of the event onto the screen. Then the points for each team. No event name or competitors name or performances are written down. From time to time, for instance when there is a lull in the number of recording sheets to be processed, an up to date score can be obtained. The computer adds up all the scores which have been entered for each team up to that time and immediately prints them out on paper. (Figure 7.7) The paper is then given straight to the announcer without anyone having to add up these numbers or write anything down.

```
AGE GROUP SCORES


1ST YEAR SCORES
        1    DUNDRY           0034 POINTS
        2    MENDIP           0032 POINTS


2ND YEAR SCORES
        1    DUNDRY           0038 POINTS
        2    MENDIP           0028 POINTS


OVERALL TOTALS
        1    DUNDRY           0072 POINTS
        2    MENDIP           0060 POINTS
```

Figure 7.7
At anytime, at the press of a button an up to date score can be printed out for the announcer.

The data entered about each event is saved onto disc so that it is not lost. This means that a sports day event which might overlap lunch time or even two days can still use this program by saving the data and recalling it at a later stage.

Checks can be made as sports day progresses of the scores which have already been entered and which event recording sheets are still outstanding. The latter is particularly useful towards the end of Sports Day.

The computer can pick out individual events to check whether points have been entered or to see whether the correct points were recorded. (Figure 7.8).

```
003 2ND YEAR    100M    GIRLS
DUNDRY                  05 POINTS
MENDIP                  06 POINTS
```

Figure 7.8
Data which was entered for a particular event.

The computer will also print out the points scored in every event by each team. (Figure 7.9) This might show that for some events, like events 7 and 8, no points have been entered, in other words the result sheet has not been processed. Once the team points from the last event sheet have been entered into the computer the final score can be printed out immediately.

With the assistance of this type of computer program the Sports Day organiser can cease to worry over the prompt and accurate analysis of the results.

Figure 7.9
Points which have been entered for every event.

```
001 1ST YEAR    100M    GIRLS
DUNDRY                  08 POINTS
MENDIP                  03 POINTS

002 1ST YEAR    100M    BOYS
DUNDRY                  04 POINTS
MENDIP                  07 POINTS

003 2ND YEAR    100M    GIRLS
DUNDRY                  05 POINTS
MENDIP                  06 POINTS

004 2ND YEAR    100M    BOYS
DUNDRY                  07 POINTS
MENDIP                  04 POINTS

005 1ST YEAR    L.J.    GIRLS
DUNDRY                  03 POINTS
MENDIP                  08 POINTS

006 1ST YEAR    L.J.    BOYS
DUNDRY                  06 POINTS
MENDIP                  05 POINTS

007 2ND YEAR    L.J.    GIRLS
DUNDRY                  00 POINTS
MENDIP                  00 POINTS

008 2ND YEAR    L.J.    BOYS
DUNDRY                  00 POINTS
MENDIP                  00 POINTS

009 1ST YEAR    SHOT    GIRLS
DUNDRY                  07 POINTS
MENDIP                  04 POINTS

010 1ST YEAR    SHOT    BOYS
DUNDRY                  06 POINTS
MENDIP                  05 POINTS
```

Sports Day

4. SCHOOL RECORDS

Part of the reason why we run a sports day event is to allow for, encourage and admire the pursuit of excellence. Previous athletic records are the source of inspiration which motivate the next young generation of athletes to greater achievements. An essential element of the pre-sports day 'general information' which is circulated to all pupils must be the publication of the current school athletics records.

Producing an up to date list need no longer consist of a hand written piece of paper with various names and performances crossed out covering the past few years. Records should be kept on computer for ease of sorting, printing and up-dating. A database program is the best method of holding and amending such data. The method is similar to the way the entries were handled.

The database is set up with a certain number of fields which will contain the basic information for each record. Nine fields are used to cover:

1. NUM   a special order number for printing purposes
2. YR   the age group of competition, 1st Year, 2nd Year etc
3. WHO   gender of event, girls or boys
4. EVENT   name of event, 100M, SHOT etc
5. NAME   surname followed by initial to obtain alphabetical order
6. HOUSE   or Tutor Group or School depending on the event
7. YEAR   the year in which the record was achieved
8. PERFORM   the performance achieved
9. NO   the event number as per programme and event recording sheets

Once all the records have been entered into the computer (figure 7.10) it is possible to extract the data in ways which would never be considered from a hand written or even typed list. This would be particularly true for a school sports day where there might be around 100 records.

The records can be re-ordered so that they appear in say alphabetical surname order (Figure 7.11). Here the names can be checked to see how many pupils hold more than one record.

A list can be arranged in 'age' order to identify

```
SPORTS DAY RECORDS - EVENT ORDER
--------------------------------------------------

NO YR  WHO   EVENT NAME      HOUSE  YEAR PERFORM
--  --  ----  ----- ----     -----  ---- -------
 1 1YR GIRLS 100M  SMITH K   MENDIP 1985 14.32 SECS
 2 1YR BOYS  100M  BROWN D   MENDIP 1982 13.88 SECS
 3 2YR GIRLS 100M  GREEN F   DUNDRY 1986 14.12 SECS
 4 2YR BOYS  100M  YELLOW J  MENDIP 1983 13.52 SECS
 5 1YR GIRLS L.J.  BLUE  E   DUNDRY 1985  3.87 METRES
 6 1YR BOYS  L.J.  JONES L   DUNDRY 1982  4.31 METRES
 7 2YR GIRLS L.J.  LEWIS J   MENDIP 1986  4.68 METRES
 8 2YR BOYS  L.J.  RED   T   MENDIP 1983  4.79 METRES
 9 1YR GIRLS SHOT  COX   F   MENDIP 1984  7.73 METRES
10 1YR BOYS  SHOT  DAY   I   DUNDRY 1985  8.16 METRES
11 2YR GIRLS SHOT  NIGHT T   DUNDRY 1983  7.98 METRES
12 2YR BOYS  SHOT  FRY   W   MENDIP 1986 10.23 METRES
```

Figure 7.10
Sports Day records held in a database.

```
SPORTS DAY RECORDS - ALPHABETICAL SURNAME ORDER
--------------------------------------------------

NAME       YR  WHO   EVENT HOUSE  YEAR PERFORM
----       --  ----  ----- -----  ---- -------
BLUE  E   1YR GIRLS L.J.  DUNDRY 1985  3.87 METRES
BROWN D   1YR BOYS  100M  MENDIP 1982 13.88 SECS
COX   F   1YR GIRLS SHOT  MENDIP 1984  7.73 METRES
DAY   I   1YR BOYS  SHOT  DUNDRY 1985  8.16 METRES
FRY   W   2YR BOYS  SHOT  MENDIP 1986 10.23 METRES
GREEN F   2YR GIRLS 100M  DUNDRY 1986 14.12 METRES
JONES L   1YR BOYS  L.J.  DUNDRY 1982  4.31 METRES
LEWIS J   2YR GIRLS L.J.  MENDIP 1986  4.68 METRES
NIGHT T   2YR GIRLS SHOT  DUNDRY 1983  7.98 METRES
RED   T   2YR BOYS  L.J.  MENDIP 1983  4.79 METRES
SMITH K   1YR GIRLS 100M  MENDIP 1985 14.32 SECS
YELLOW J  2YR BOYS  100M  MENDIP 1983 13.52 SECS
```

Figure 7.11
The records can be sorted into alphabetical surname order.

the oldest and longest standing records as well as the most recent ones. (Figure 7.12).

The computer is able to extract selected data which is particularly important for that pre-sports day information. It could print out the records

Figure 7.12
It is easy to identify old records by sorting the list according to the year in which it was achieved.

```
SPORTS DAY RECORDS - YEAR ORDER
--------------------------------------------------

YEAR YR  WHO   EVENT NAME      HOUSE  PERFORM
---- --  ----  ----- ----     -----  -------
1982 1YR BOYS  100M  BROWN D   MENDIP 13.88 SECS
1982 1YR BOYS  L.J.  JONES L   DUNDRY  4.31 METRES
1983 2YR GIRLS SHOT  NIGHT T   DUNDRY  7.98 METRES
1983 2YR BOYS  L.J.  RED   T   MENDIP  4.79 METRES
1983 2YR BOYS  100M  YELLOW J  MENDIP 13.52 SECS
1984 1YR GIRLS SHOT  COX   F   MENDIP  7.73 METRES
1985 1YR GIRLS L.J.  BLUE  E   DUNDRY  3.87 METRES
1985 1YR BOYS  SHOT  DAY   I   DUNDRY  8.16 METRES
1985 1YR GIRLS 100M  SMITH K   MENDIP 14.32 SECS
1986 2YR BOYS  SHOT  FRY   W   MENDIP 10.23 METRES
1986 2YR GIRLS 100M  GREEN F   DUNDRY 14.12 SECS
1986 2YR GIRLS L.J.  LEWIS J   MENDIP  4.68 METRES
```

held in just the First Year Girls events (figure 7.13) or all the records held by just 2nd Year pupils. (Figure 7.l4) House staff would be interested in the records held by their pupils and

```
SPORTS DAY RECORDS FOR 1ST YEAR GIRLS
-------------------------------------

YR  WHO    EVENT NAME    HOUSE   PERFORM      YEAR
-------------------------------------------------
1YR GIRLS L.J.   BLUE E   DUNDRY   3.87 METRES 1985
1YR GIRLS SHOT   COX F    MENDIP   7.73 METRES 1984
1YR GIRLS 100M   SMITH K  MENDIP  14.32 SECS   1985
```

Figure 7.13
Selected records for 1st Year Girls.

```
2ND YEAR SPORTS DAY RECORDS
---------------------------

WHO    EVENT NAME    HOUSE   PERFORM      YEAR
---------------------------------------------
BOYS   SHOT  FRY W    MENDIP 10.23 METRES 1986
GIRLS  100M  GREEN F  DUNDRY 14.12 SECS   1986
GIRLS  L.J.  LEWIS J  MENDIP  4.68 METRES 1986
GIRLS  SHOT  NIGHT T  DUNDRY  7.98 METRES 1983
BOYS   L.J.  RED T    MENDIP  4.79 METRES 1983
BOYS   100M  YELLOW J MENDIP 13.52 SECS   1983
```

Figure 7.14
All Sports Day records for a Year Group.

figure 7.l5 shows those records held by pupils in Dundry House.

The task of producing a new list of records following a Sports Day event is a quick and easy job. It involves editing the records database by changing only four items of data for each record broken, the pupil's name along with their performance, house and the calendar year. New lists can be printed out and displayed immediately without having to re-write anything or have the office staff re-type the whole document. Why wait until next year to display the current situation when up to date athletics records could be on

Figure 7.15
All Sports Day records held by one House.

```
ALL RECORDS HELD BY PUPILS FROM DUNDRY HOUSE
--------------------------------------------

YR  WHO   EVENT NAME    PERFORM      YEAR
-----------------------------------------
1YR BOYS  L.J.  JONES L   4.31 METRES 1982
2YR GIRLS SHOT  NIGHT T   7.98 METRES 1983
1YR GIRLS L.J.  BLUE E    3.87 METRES 1985
1YR BOYS  SHOT  DAY I     8.16 METRES 1985
2YR GIRLS 100M  GREEN F  14.12 SECS   1986
```

the notice board the morning after Sports Day.

An extract from this new list can be printed showing the new records. (Figure 7.16) A copy of this could be given to the Head to announce in assembly the next day along with the printed final result.

```
SPORTS DAY RECORDS ACHIEVED IN 1986
-----------------------------------

YR   WHO   EVENT NAME    HOUSE   PERFORM
---------------------------------------
2YR BOYS   SHOT  FRY W    MENDIP 10.23 METRES
2YR GIRLS  100M  GREEN F  DUNDRY 14.12 SECS
2YR GIRLS  L.J.  LEWIS J  MENDIP  4.68 METRES
```

Figure 7.16
Records achieved in a single year.

5. RESULTS PUBLICATION

Many organisers of athletic events will be content simply to pin up the event result sheets on the day for the athletes to view rather than be faced with the massive administrative task of producing a comprehensive results publication.

The results can be published in two forms using the computer. The database program which collected and printed out the entries could be adapted to take details of performances as well. However, it would take a relatively long time on the computer to access the names of those in an event, insert their performance, sort out that data into order of finish and print out the result. It could be done this way but it is inefficient and what we are seeking are ways of using the computer that are better than methods we previously employed.

A specially written computer program which would accept and sort out the entries and also handle the results has already been mentioned. Such a program would enable the teacher to insert the performances for each competitor in every event. This would be much quicker and would produce the type of results athletes and spectators want to see. Such print outs could be collated like the entries to be photo-copied into a publication containing all the results. (Figure 7.l7).

The use of a computer during Sports Day will reduce the work-load on the day by both the organiser and the recorders. It will help to provide a better commentary from the announcer who can be given full details of all event records

Sports Day

```
----------------------------------------------
RESULT OF YEAR 1   BOYS 100M
----------------------------------------------
1st  DAW TERRY     MENDIP    14.83 secs
2nd  WHITE IAN     DUNDRY    15.62 secs
3rd  SMITH SIMON   DUNDRY    15.88 secs
4th  HAND LEE      MENDIP    16.02 secs
----------------------------------------------


----------------------------------------------------------
RESULT OF YEAR 2   GIRLS LONG JUMP
----------------------------------------------------------
1st  GREEN JUNE   MENDIP   4.34 : 4.77 : 4.10 -*- 4.77 METRES
2nd  FORD LIZ     DUNDRY   3.92 : 4.05 : 3.83 -*- 4.05 METRES
3rd  BLACK EMMA   MENDIP   3.88 : 3.92 : 2.93 -*- 3.92 METRES
4th  KNEE HELEN   DUNDRY   3.53 : 2.23 : 3.01 -*- 3.53 METRES
----------------------------------------------------------
```

Figure 7.17
Sports Day Results.

along with the names of all competitors before sports day begins. The spectators will receive a more frequent up date of the team scores and they will get the final result announced much more quickly than during previous events.

When preparing for Sports Day don't forget to add the computer to the list of essential equipment required, as well as the stop watches, relay batons and other paraphernalia!.

Fitness Work

Fitness work has assumed a more prominent role in the physical education curriculum in recent years with the introduction of schemes to promote health related fitness. Fitness is not a new concept for as long ago as 1909 the Board of Education Syllabus of Physical Exercises mentions that ...

"One of the aims of Physical Training is to promote the development of the muscular system and the body as a whole, in order to attain the highest possible degree of all-round physical fitness".

Any book on 'fitness', particularly American ones, will reveal a vast array of methods of achieving a high level of fitness. The evaluation of levels of fitness has led to many tests being developed this century.

The testing and measuring of pupil performance should only be carried out in schools if it can be carried out efficiently. Testing and measuring should not be used as a substitute for teaching and the teacher should not be seen as merely a timekeeper, measurer or recording machine but actively involved in the teaching of what fitness is all about and why it is important.

Some fitness tests have their problems for schools as they require costly and complicated equipment which is more often found and used today only in institutes of higher education. But there are many simplified tests which are well suited for school use.

Problems do arise when it comes to working out the results of some of these test because the tables are too complicated for the pupils to use or understand. Writing out the results and feeding back information to the pupils as to what those results mean can be very time consuming and therefore, regretably, these tasks may not occur at all.

Fitness work should be a definite planned part of the physical education curriculum for all pupils. The object should be to make pupils aware of the importance and necessity of fitness. It should not be a programme devoted to competition to see who is the fittest but one which demonstrates the benefits and value of exercise for a fit and healthy lifestyle. Implementing a scheme of work on fitness will require careful and thoughtful planning. Let us examine a scheme which includes some weight training, circuit training and running as a means of looking at ways of getting fit and ways of keeping fit.

It is not sufficient simply to ask the pupils to participate in these activities without there being some record kept of their performances and some form of evaluation of their progress throughout the programme. Two forms of evaluation should take place.

Firstly, individual performances in each of the three activitites should be monitored. Providing the run uses the same course, pupils can test themselves against the clock. Pupils can be timed over a circuit in the gym using standardised instruction cards on the gym wall detailing the required repetitions for each exercise. The recording of weight being lifted and the number of repetitions achieved can be carried out using standard weight lifting equipment or a multi-gym.

For the second part of the evaluation, there ought to be some measure of the overall changes in levels of fitness which might occur during the course of operating this scheme. What is needed is a general fitness test which can be carried out fairly quickly, hopefully in one lesson, so that an assessment of each pupils' level of fitness can be obtained. Ideally, if pupils were working to improve their knowledge as well as their own personal level of fitness, then an evaluation of their level of fitness both at the start and at the end of the programme is essential.

Fitness Work

Whilst physical educationists would accept that any true measurement of 'fitness' ought to take into account the cardiovascular component, it may be more important at school level to find a fitness test which is quick and easy to administer to a whole class group. As many lower ability pupils are unable to take their pulse rates accurately a simple test which would give an INDICATION of their levels of fitness will be acceptable. Departmental capitation may not extend to the purchase of expensive and sophisticated monitoring equipment to analyse such cardiovasular information.

By using a test like the JCR fitness test it is possible to assess a whole teaching group within a one hour lesson. The JCR test is a three-item motor fitness test in which pupils have to carry out a standing high jump, perform maximum chins to the beam and be timed over a ten by

Picture 8.1
The JCR fitness test: the jump with computer for analysing the scores.

ten yard shuttle run. Although the test does not include cardiovasular measurements directly it was designed to measure elements of fitness such as strength, speed, agility and endurance.

Once all three tests have been completed the three performances are converted to points from a table, added together and then compared with a fitness grading chart. The tables and analysis are rather complex and it would take the teacher two evenings to analyse and write out the results for one class. When this happens the pupils may not get their scores until the following week.

Part of the solution to many of these problems is to seek the assistance of a computer. The writing of a JCR fitness test analysis computer program solves the two main problems of this sort of testing.

Firstly, many lower ability pupils are able to self-administer the actual physical part of the tests but are unable to understand the analysis tables. The computer program does away with the need for anyone to consult such tables.

Secondly, the use of a computer program has to enable a class being tested to produce their results on paper within a one hour lesson. Giving out the results the following week is a disaster in terms of motivation and feed back.

The JCR test was first established in 1947 by N.C. Cooper and later adapted by B.E. Phillips in 1963. Each age group have their own set of points for each activity although there is a common fitness grading score for all ages. This meant that as a pupil grows older they have to perform significantly better to score the same number of points.

In writing the JCR computer program the scoring system was modified so that there was a common scoring system for performance, regardless of age, so that improved performance over time was rewarded by increased points. To achieve a comparable grade each age group have to score more points than they achieved in previous year.

The JCR program is an integrated computer program which links in with the Year File program (see chapter 4). This means that there is no need for anyone to write out any pupil names as these details are obtained from the pupil data created by the Year File and stored on disc.

At the beginning of the lesson the computer, a

monitor, disc drive and a printer are set up in the gymnasium along with the other equipment for the test. The pupils work in pairs and check each other on the three activities and record their performances on sheets of paper. The JCR program will generate recording sheets using the pupil data from the Year File to create lists of pupils along with spaces for their performance details. (Figure 8.1) When the pupils have completed all three activities they can then go to the computer.

```
+-------------------------------------------------------------+
! PUPIL REFERENCE NUMBERS AND RECORDING SHEET                 !
! FOR 3rd YEAR PUPILS.                                        !
+-------------------------------------------------------------+
! No. ! NAME                   ! T/G    ! JUMP ! CHINS ! RUN  !
+-------------------------------------------------------------+
! 026 ! DAVID BARRINGTON       ! 3SKI   !      !       !      !
! 010 ! ANDREW BUSH            ! 3HAR   !      !       !      !
! 001 ! JAMIE CROSS            ! 3BARN  !      !       !      !
! 017 ! MICHAEL EDGAR          ! 3HOB   !      !       !      !
! 027 ! DONALD FORD            ! 3SKI   !      !       !      !
! 012 ! JEFFREY GAMAN          ! 3HAR   !      !       !      !
! 003 ! STEVEN HARVEY          ! 3BARN  !      !       !      !
! 030 ! SHANE HOBBS            ! 3SKI   !      !       !      !
! 005 ! DAVID HUGHES           ! 3BARN  !      !       !      !
! 014 ! ANDREW LEWIS           ! 3HAR   !      !       !      !
! 031 ! NEIL PAYNE             ! 3SKI   !      !       !      !
! 022 ! PAUL RUSH              ! 3HOB   !      !       !      !
! 016 ! DARREN SUTTON          ! 3HAR   !      !       !      !
! 023 ! KEITH THOMPSON         ! 3HOB   !      !       !      !
! 007 ! GERRY VOLLERO          ! 3BARN  !      !       !      !
! 024 ! PAUL WAGLAND           ! 3HOB   !      !       !      !
+-------------------------------------------------------------+
```

Figure 8.1
JCR Fitness Test Recording Sheet produced by the computer program.

Each pupil has to entered FIVE pieces of information, all numerical. Firstly they key in their Year by number and then their pupil reference number. This is the same reference number which they keep throughout the school which is allocated to them by the Year File when they first enter the school. The reference number system saves a great deal of time as pupils do not have to write out their full name on the keyboard.

The pupil then enters the three performances which they achieved in the jump, chin and run tests. Once all this data has been entered an immediate print out of all performances, scores and fitness grade is obtained. The results can be seen on the monitor but it is also sent straight to the printer for a hard copy on paper. (Figure 8.2) This means that there is no need for a pupil to dwell on their results by looking at the monitor as they can be given the information on paper from the printer. These results could be printed on NCR paper if the teacher wanted a copy as well as giving the pupils their copy to keep.

```
+-------------------------------------------------------------+
| ANDREW BUSH OF 3HAR                                         |
|                                                             |
| JUMP    12 Inches.    JUMP SCORE    026                     |
|                                                             |
| CHINS 06 Scored.  CHINS SCORE   068                         |
|                                                             |
| RUNS    28 Seconds   RUNS SCORE    040                      |
|                                                             |
|                TOTAL POINTS SCORED 134                      |
|                                                             |
| ACHIEVED A GRADE 4 ACCORDING TO                             |
| THE FOLLOWING FITNESS SCALES FOR                            |
| 3rd YEAR PUPILS.                                            |
|                                                             |
|         GRADE 1    OVER 226                                 |
|         GRADE 2    180 TO 225                               |
|         GRADE 3    151 TO 179                               |
|         GRADE 4    123 TO 150                               |
|         GRADE 5    90 TO 122                                |
|         GRADE 6    BELOW 90                                 |
+-------------------------------------------------------------+
```

Figure 8.2
The print out which each pupil receives as soon as they have finished their JCR test.

This system frees the computer so that the next pupil can enter their details straight away. On average a pupil will spend 20 seconds on the computer, at most 30 seconds depending on their level of keyboard skills. A class of 30 pupils can all have their printed results in their hands within 15 minutes, rather better than the following week.

Throughout this time the teacher is totally free to give assistance where necessary during the testing and to explain the meaning of the results as they come off the printer. Because of the instant result service, interest and motivation is dramatically increased and levels of performance are higher. Some pupils even go back to try to improve their scores to get those few extra points for the next grade.

During the lesson the computer will store all the data being entered by each pupil. At the end

Fitness Work

Picture 8.2
The JCR fitness test: the chins.

Testing can be carried out by devoting one lesson to it at the beginning of the Autumn term or by incorporating it into a planned scheme of work on fitness for all pupils. It can be used at the beginning and end of a 'fitness' scheme of work to assess changes which might have occurred as a result of their fitness programme.

Just testing is not enough. Something should also be done with all the data which is collected from each test. Pupils do of course get their individual print-out of their test performance and the teacher can get a group summary.

But by using other computer programs it is possible to carry out two other functions with all this data. With a database program, it is possible to first store the performance results of an individual over a five year period and second to carry out some statistical analysis of the group data.

Pupil records can be built up over the years of all the scores achieved in each JCR testing session. These can then be printed out and presented to the pupil in the fifth year. (Figure 8.4)

of the session the teacher can obtain a print out containing a summary of all the scores and grades for each pupil. (Figure 8.3) The data can be stored on disc for a future occasion. This would allow for a whole year group to be tested on different occasions.

No.	NAME AND T/G	JUMP	SCORE	CHINS	SCORE	RUN	SCORE	TOTAL	GRADE
026	DAVID BARRINGTON of 3SKI	15	50	10	90	25	72	212	2/6
010	ANDREW BUSH of 3HAR	12	26	6	68	28	40	134	4/6
001	JAMIE CROSS of 3BARN	8	8	5	62	30	24	94	5/6
017	MICHAEL EDGAR of 3HOB	14	40	3	50	33	16	106	5/6
027	DONALD FORD of 3SKI	9	12	2	38	38	6	56	6/6
012	JEFFREY GAMAN of 3HAR	18	78	12	94	25	72	244	1/6
003	STEVEN HARVEY of 3BARN	0	0	0	0	0	0	0	0/6
030	SHANE HOBBS of 3SKI	12	26	2	38	29	30	94	5/6
005	DAVID HUGHES of 3BARN	10	16	5	62	28	40	118	5/6
014	ANDREW LEWIS of 3HAR	17	70	15	97	24	82	249	1/6
031	NEIL PAYNE of 3SKI	16	60	14	96	26	60	216	2/6
022	PAUL RUSH of 3HOB	15	50	12	94	26	60	204	2/6
016	DARREN SUTTON of 3HAR	0	0	0	0	0	0	0	0/6
023	KEITH THOMPSON of 3HOB	15	50	9	84	30	24	158	3/6
007	GERRY VOLLERO of 3BARN	13	32	6	68	31	20	120	5/6
024	PAUL WAGLAND of 3HOB	9	12	17	99	27	50	161	3/6

Figure 8.3
The summary for the teacher of all performances and grades achieved by each pupil.

Testing all pupils at the beginning of every school year becomes a feasable project with the aid of this JCR computer program. This would also compliment other work being carried out in physical education lessons in explaining the necessity and the importance of physical fitness.

This long term evaluation enables the pupils to see any changes in their fitness scores whilst they are at school with the results forming the basis of a five year pupil fitness profile. It should always be emphasised that fitness testing should be carried out against oneself and not, although it cannot be prevented, against others in the class.

```
------------------------------------------------

JCR FITNESS TEST RESULTS

NAME:     JIMMY SMITH

YEAR      JUMP    CHINS   RUN    POINTS  GRADE

YEAR 1    12      3       23     186     3

YEAR 2    13      4       23     200     3

YEAR 3    13      4       22     206     3

YEAR 4    15      6       22     240     3

YEAR 5    17      10      21     302     2

------------------------------------------------
```

Figure 8.4
The JCR test scores achieved by a pupil over a five year period.

Details of performances in various other fitness tests can be added to the JCR record. Here the aim is to produce a 'composite fitness grade' based on a wider selection of tests. Data from such testing could be combined into a much larger 'Fitness Profile' for every pupil over a five year period. (Figure 8.5).

```
-----------------------------------------------

FITNESS PROFILE

NAME:    JIMMY SMITH

                      YEAR
FITNESS TEST     1   2   3   4   5

JCR              3   3   3   3   2
12 MIN.RUN       5   5   4   4   4
CROSS COUNTRY    6   5   5   4   4
HEXAGONAL TEST   4   3   3   3   2
SIT UPS          3   2   2   2   1
STANDING L.J.    4   3   2   2   2
BALANCE TEST     6   6   5   4   4

COMPOSITE
FITNESS GRADE    4   4   3   3   3

-----------------------------------------------
```

Figure 8.5
A composite pupil fitness profile over a five year period.

Part of the problem of using several different established or self-devised fitness tests is the different grading systems or assessment schemes which each one adopts. Some are based upon percentiles, others on a 'Good', 'Average' and 'Poor' scale, others on a five or six point alphabetical or numerical grade. Relating levels of performance across a range of uncon-nected tests is very confusing for the pupils.

When establishing a battery of fitness tests it is important that the system is suitable for the school. The tests do not necessarily have to be very sophisticated nor require expensive monitoring equipment to get over the principle to the pupils that some form of 'evaluation' is essential when considering aspects of fitness. The teacher has to take into account the length of time available for testing and consider how much of the topic of fitness is going to be carried out by demonstration and how much will be experienced practically by all pupils.

Basic exercises like press ups, sit ups, standing long jump, shuttle runs or sit and reach tests can all be carried out with little or no equipment or expense. But to link these together in some form of meaningful battery of tests and establish a common grading system for each one might prove a daunting task for any Physical Education teacher without the aid of a computer.

The statistical analysis options of a database program can be used to analyse group data quickly so that grades can be established to suit the performances of pupils in a school.

A school might decide to establish a six point grading system in their fitness tests. First, data is obtained from a group of pupils who have taken part in say two tests, a timed run and a timed hexagonal test. The latter is used in skiing to test

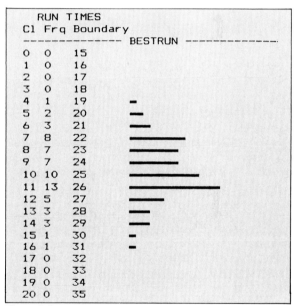

Figure 8.6
A bar chart showing the pupil performances in the running test.

coordination, balance and fitness by jumping around a hexagonal shape. The data is fed into a database which generates bar charts for each test. (Figures 8.6 and 8.7) These show a near normal distribution but how can they be changed to the required six point scale.

The database can be programmed to calculate the Mean and Standard Deviation for each test:

RUN TIMES		HEX TEST	
Mean	25.0 mins	Mean	14.3 secs
S.D.	2.5 mins	S.D	3.3 secs

Fitness Work

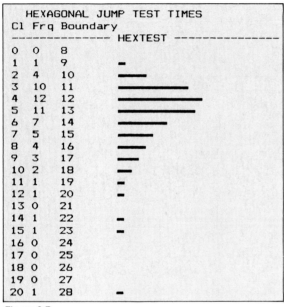

Figure 8.7
A bar chart showing the pupil performances in the jump test.

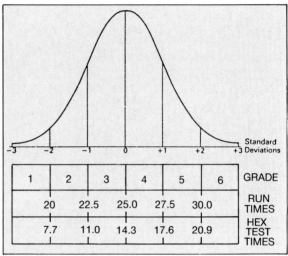

Figure 8.8
A normal curve showing how our results can be converted into grades for the two tests.

A normal curve of distribution can be divided into six segments, or standards, three on each side of the mean. (Figure 8.8) This can be the basis for the six grades.

RUN TIMES		HEX TEST	
TIMES	GRADE	TIMES	GRADE
Less than 20 mins	1	Less than 7.7 secs	1
20.0 → 22.4	2	7.7 → 10.9	2
22.5 → 24.9	3	11.0 → 14.2	3
25.0 → 27.4	4	14.3 → 17.5	4
27.5 → 29.9	5	17.6 → 20.8	5
30.0 or greater	6	20.9 or greater	6

These grades and corresponding performance limits could then become part of a computer program which would automatically indicate the grade, as in the JCR program. Once the grading is determined the group data can be checked by re-running the bar chart program. (Figures 8.9 and 8.10) Instead of using a general scale the new grading figures should be used. On examination, the revised chart for the run shows clearly the six blocks representing grades one to six. The Hexagonal test needs a little more interpretation. There is one very high time, 28.88

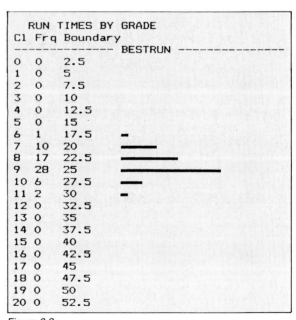

Figure 8.9
The restructured bar chart shows the distribution of grades achieved in the running test.

secs, but this would still count as a grade six even though it was more than three standard deviations away from the mean. At the other end

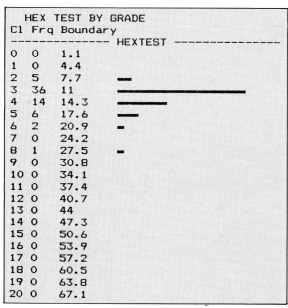

```
   HEX TEST BY GRADE
  Cl Frq Boundary
  -------------- HEXTEST ---------------
   0   0   1.1
   1   0   4.4
   2   5   7.7    ━━
   3  36   11     ━━━━━━━━━━━━━━━━━━━━━
   4  14   14.3   ━━━━━━━━
   5   6   17.6   ━━━
   6   2   20.9   ▪
   7   0   24.2
   8   1   27.5   ▪
   9   0   30.8
  10   0   34.1
  11   0   37.4
  12   0   40.7
  13   0   44
  14   0   47.3
  15   0   50.6
  16   0   53.9
  17   0   57.2
  18   0   60.5
  19   0   63.8
  20   0   67.1
```

Figure 8.10
The restructured bar chart shows the distribution of grades achieved in the jump test.

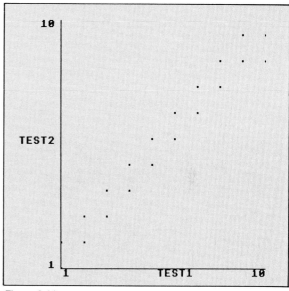

Figure 8.11
A scattergram showing a high degree of correlation between two fitness tests.

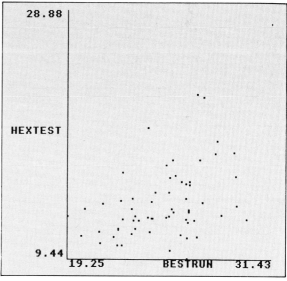

Figure 8.12
No correlation is apparent when comparing these two tests.

of the scale there are no times within the grade one catagory of less than 7.7 secs so the best pupil performances would be classified as a grade 2.

In establishing grading schemes for a variety of 'fitness tests' and by storing all the data, comparisons can then be made between any two sets of data. To test the correlation between two sets of fitness test data would be a long and complex calculation by 'hand'. Using the computer the two sets of data are recalled from the disc and a correllation diagram can be produced within seconds.

To achieve a high degree of correlation the graph would need to show a distribution in a straight line away from the 'ZERO' point. Figure 8.11 illustrates a near perfect correlation. It would be no surprise to find that pupils who achieved a high grade in the JCR test also achieved a high grade in the Cooper 12 minute running test; a good correlation.

The wider the distribution the less the correlation. There would not necessarily be any expected correlation between times achieved on a run with times for the Hexagonal jump test. (Figure 8.12).

Figure 8.13 indicates a negative correlation although in fitness terms we would not expect

Fitness Work

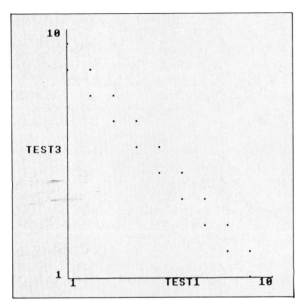

Figure 8.13
This scattergram shows a negative correlation.

this to occur. It is normal for a pupil who is generally regarded as being 'fit' to achieve high scores in nearly all tests carried out. Similarly, pupils who might be considered 'unfit' score poorly in most tests.

There are other ways of analysing this type of data, for instance, a four or five point grading scheme could be established instead of the six. Calculations can be made by the computer as results are being fed in so that the teachers summary (figure 8.3) could also show details of the mean, standard deviation, highest score and lowest score for that particular group.

OTHER TESTS

Computer programs can be written to help analyse any type of fitness test. Many schools could write their own programs for fitness tests which they regularly use. If P.E. staff are unable to embark upon such writing then there may be pupils who are taking computer studies who might be able to write these programs as part of their computer studies examination project.

A relatively simple project would be to write a program to determine the fitness rating for the Havard Step Test. The resting pulse rate followed

by the other pulse readings would be fed into the computer after the required period of exercise. The computer would then use those figures in the Step Test formulae to produce the fitness rating.

Chosing a fitness test to suit your own school and pupils is a most important factor. With the aid of a computer, fitness testing can be made more efficient by producing these 'instant' results. Storing and using the data to feed back information to the pupils should be an essential part of any fitness testing work. New ways are being developed so that data from fitness tests can not only be automatically analysed to produce a fitness grade but also be placed straight into a database program for storing and further analysis.

Instead of relying on pupils to take their own pulse rate it is possible to obtain sensors which are attached to the body and linked to a computer. The frequency of the pulse rate can be displayed on a monitor and as a pupil starts working, say on an exercise bike, the changes in pulse rate will appear. The information collected can be stored and analysed as before. The availability and cost of this type of equipment is gradually coming within the range of schools. It will provide the P.E. teacher with a more

Picture 8.3
Monitoring heart rate on the exercise bike.

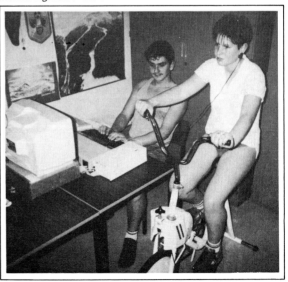

meaningful demonstration lesson on the effects of exercise to such organs as the heart and lungs.

Monitors have been developed which can be strapped to the body to collect data without being connected directly to a computer. There are two types. One in which the user can pre-program the instrument with a high and a low heart rate limit and an alarm will sound if those limits are exceeded. The second is one in which physiological data is collected and saved by the instrument whilst the user is out, say on a run. This data can then be fed into and analysed by a computer on return from a work-out.

The Eurofit PWC170 test is designed to calculates the percentage of body fat, lean body mass and physical work capacity (PWC). There is now a computer program to help in the analysis of the data. Personal data is first entered into the computer followed by the skin fold measurements from which the percentage of body fat and lean body mass is estimated. For the PWC test, options on loading and timing are decided before work commences on the exercise bike. Heart rates are entered after each phase and at the end of the test a print out will reproduce all the data which has been entered as well as provide a detailed analysis of the results. All this information can be stored on disc and recalled later.

In the area of fitness, and especially in fitness testing, the computer is a useful tool to provide quick and accurate results.

Fitness Work

Cross Country Race Analysis
Triathlon and Orienteering

Picture 9.1
The computer can be used for cross country race analysis.

A cross country event, especially one with a large number of runners, can impose a heavy workload on the organiser both before and during the race. However, the pressure can be eased considerably by using the computer to assist with all the different aspects and stages of organising a cross country event. This includes all the initial administrative tasks as well as the result analysis.

Although a cross country event may be organised in a variety of ways, and these will be looked at later, essentially there are a number of elements which each event organiser has to cover regardless of the type of event. Such elements include:

1. The production and distribution of the race information.
2. Entry forms.
3. Instructions to officials.
4. Race recording sheets.
5. Race analysis.

RACE INFORMATION

A general information sheet about a cross country event has to be circulated to all concerned, whether it is for the County Championships or an Inter House race at a school. People have to be informed or reminded

Cross Country Race Analysis

of some basic race details. However, these basic facts are invariably the same each year. Such items as the age groups, the number of pupils allowed to run, the teams involved, the scoring system, the details about how runners will be numbered, if that applies, and, if it is a school event, the details of the course, will all remain the same each year. Only the date of the event will need to be changed and perhaps the venue if it is a County or inter school event.

Each year the organiser would look back at the previous years' race details, amend the date and either re-write it completely or ask the school secretary to re-type it all once more. By using the computer with a word processor all the race information can be stored on disc and recalled each year. When it is time to start preparations for the next cross country season the disc from the previous year is located and the general race information data is loaded back into the word processor. Amendments are made, such as the change of date, and a new printed master copy of the information sheet is produced for duplication on the school photo-copier and subsequent distribution. (Figure 9.1)

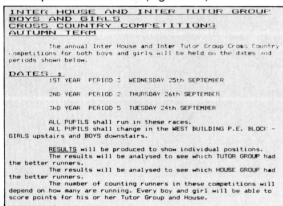

Figure 9.1
The word processed information sheet with only the date needing amending each year.

ENTRY FORMS

If entry forms are required these too could be produced on the word processor with a similar ability to have the date and venue inserted each year before being duplicated. (Figure 9.2)

INSTRUCTIONS TO OFFICIALS

Some cross country courses are of a quite

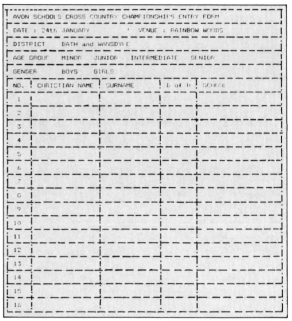

Figure 9.2
An entry form for the County Championships produced on the word processor.

complicated design, especially if it is a County event where there might be six or eight events all of different lengths and consisting of a variety of loops according to the distance required for each race. The instructions for the officials for such an event are invariably long and complicated but have to be very thorough to avoid any ambiguity and confusion once the races start.

The organiser can make things easier for himself by using the same course each year but even so instructions for a race may run to several pages in length. By writing out these instructions on the word processor they can be stored on disc and recalled and re-printed like the general information sheet each year. This in itself saves an enormous amount of writing time and even if the venue was changed these instructions could be easily and quickly amended for the new course.

RECORDING SHEETS

The main thing about organising a cross country event is to ensure that as much work as possible is carried out BEFORE the day of the event. Names of runners must be known beforehand whether it is a small or a large event that is being organised. Names and teams can then be entered into special computer programs which can be made to perform a number of tasks for the organiser, depending on the event.

Let us examine two different types of cross country event and see how the computer can be used in each. These two events will be first a school inter house and inter tutor group competition and secondly a County Championship event.

Many schools will arrange races for a whole year group of pupils who are administratively organised into a Tutor Group as well as a House system. With this system it is possible to have three competitons in the one race, i.e. an individual race, upon which is based an inter tutor group competition as well as an inter house competition. Some schools may have only one of the latter two competitions but the principles that follow are the same.

The whole year should be asked to run in such cross country races to achieve maximum participation. This will avoid the necessity to obtain 'entries' and it will enable the teacher to access all the pupil names for each race from the Year File computer program described earlier (Chapter 4). By going to that program and asking for an alphabetical sort, followed by a sort into boys and then girls, an alphabetical list of each sex can be saved on disc. Before completing that sort it is essential to check that the Year File is up to date and that any new pupil has been entered otherwise they will not appear on the lists.

This data will then be used first to produce a recording sheet and secondly for the race analysis so avoiding the need to write out any pupil names. If only a certain number of runners are to compete in each team race then it may be easier to use the existing list of all pupils in the Year File and delete those who are NOT running rather than create a new file containing the names, tutor groups and houses of all those who are actually taking part.

Preferably the day before, but certainly not minutes before the race, that pupil data on disc can be fed into a computer program which will produce a recording sheet for use at the end of the cross country race. To speed up recording more than one copy of the recording sheet could

be made.

The recording sheet lists all the pupils in alphabetical order and shows their reference number, their tutor group and has a space for their race position. The system is based upon each runner at the end of the funnel being given a card, metal disc or sticker marked with their finishing position. The runner then reports to a team manager or race official to have their position recorded (Figure 9.3). There could be two or three people taking these details who have been given copies of the recording sheet mentioned above. This will decrease the time a

Figure 9.3
The named recording sheet is produced by the computer leaving only the race positions to be recorded by hand.

```
! CROSS COUNTRY RECORDING SHEET       !
! FOR THE YEAR 3 GIRLS RACE           !
! ON 26TH OCTOBER                     !
-----------------------------------------
! NO.  NAME                 ! T/G  !POS!
-----------------------------------------
! 025  KATHERINE BARNES      ! SKI  ! 6 !
-----------------------------------------
! 009  LISA BEDFORD          ! HAR  ! 11 !
-----------------------------------------
! 028  TANIA FORD            ! SKI  ! 16 !
-----------------------------------------
! 011  CAROLINE FOX          ! HAR  ! 3 !
-----------------------------------------
! 002  KAREN FRY             ! BARN ! 1 !
-----------------------------------------
! 018  NICOLA GRANGER        ! HOB  ! 12 !
-----------------------------------------
! 004  TRACEY HATHAWAY       ! BARN ! 7 !
-----------------------------------------
! 029  DEBORAH HAWKES        ! SKI  ! 2 !
-----------------------------------------
! 019  JULIE HILL            ! HOB  ! 8 !
-----------------------------------------
! 013  LISA HOWARD           ! HAR  ! 4 !
-----------------------------------------
! 020  TRACEY MEACHAM        ! HOB  ! 4 !
-----------------------------------------
! 006  SHARON MIZEN          ! BARN ! 15 !
-----------------------------------------
! 015  JANE NOTTON           ! HAR  ! 5 !
-----------------------------------------
! 021  MANDY OXENHAM         ! HOB  ! 9 !
-----------------------------------------
! 032  LISA WATKINS          ! SKI  ! 13 !
-----------------------------------------
! 008  TINA WEST             ! BARN ! 10 !
-----------------------------------------
```

Cross Country Race Analysis

runner has to spend waiting to have their position recorded.

All the recorder has to do is to insert in the blank space the finishing position shown on the numbered card given to the pupil at the end of the race. Names of runners are easy to find on the recording sheet as they are listed in alphabetical surname order. No names, no tutor groups, no houses have to be written down so within a very short space of time all runners will have reported to a recorder. If the weather is wet this operation could be carried out inside the P.E. Block or changing rooms.

There are too many cross country events where runners have to wait too long to have their position recorded. This is mainly because there has been only one recorder who has had a blank sheet of paper, perhaps with numbers down one side, and they have had to write out the runners name, tutor group and house. Trying to get those details from an exhausted, young runner can take a long, long time. Many runners, especially amongst the girls, may be in some discomfort from their exertions and may need to be attended by the teachers present. If the teachers are engaged in recording then they cannot be released to look after a distressed pupil who will then be ignored.

Because of the simplicity of this system the recorders do not necessarily have to be teachers. They could be pupils, especially those pupils who, for medical reasons, may be excused cross country running. By allowing them to assist with the organisation of the event it will give them a sense of purpose rather than being a meer spectator each time. Handing out finishing cards can again be done by medically excused pupils.

Once all pupils have reported to a recorder it is a quick and easy task to produce one master copy of positions of all runners from the two or three recording lists. Pupils who have not run would be allocated a zero.

RACE ANALYSIS

A cross country race analysis program should be used to produce the required results. Such a program is fed with the same pupil data stored on disc as was used to produce the recording sheet. When this program is being used to analyse the results, pupils names will appear on the screen in the same order as on the recording sheet with a request to add the finishing position for each pupil.

Only positions are entered into the computer and even for races containing over 100 runners this task does not take very long to complete. The program will not allow the same position to be entered twice and there are ways to correct any mistakes which may have been entered due to human error!

Once all the positions have been entered into the computer the data is sorted and the results are printed out on an attached printer. The computer will first produce a complete list of the individual result in finishing order showing position, name, tutor group and house. (Figure 9.4).

```
---------------------------------------------------
! YEAR 3 GIRLS CROSS COUNTRY         !
! INDIVIDUAL RESULT                  !
! HELD ON 26TH OCTOBER               !
---------------------------------------------------
! RACE ! NAME                ! TUTOR !
! POS  !                     ! GROUP !
---------------------------------------------------
!  1   ! KAREN FRY           ! 3BARN !
!  2   ! DEBORAH HAWKES      ! 3SKI  !
!  3   ! CAROLINE FOX        ! 3HAR  !
!  4   ! TRACEY MEACHAM      ! 3HOB  !
!  5   ! JANE NOTTON         ! 3HAR  !
!  6   ! KATHERINE BARNES    ! 3SKI  !
!  7   ! TRACEY HATHAWAY     ! 3BARN !
!  8   ! JULIE HILL          ! 3HOB  !
!  9   ! MANDY OXENHAM       ! 3HOB  !
! 10   ! TINA WEST           ! 3BARN !
! 11   ! LISA BEDFORD        ! 3HAR  !
! 12   ! NICOLA GRANGER      ! 3HOB  !
! 13   ! LISA WATKINS        ! 3SKI  !
! 14   ! LISA HOWARD         ! 3HAR  !
! 15   ! SHARON MIZEN        ! 3BARN !
! 16   ! TANIA FORD          ! 3SKI  !
---------------------------------------------------
```

Figure 9.4
The Individual Result.

Race organisers who have to write out the results by hand or even have them typed usually restrict their print out to just this individual result. They would then add up the team results and attach them to the end. By using a computer program it is possible within a short space of time to have printed, not only the individual result but also the individual performances of each pupil in both the tutor group and house competitions.

The tutor group print out produces a list of pupils from each tutor group with their race position and their position in the tutor group. (Figure 9.5) Such a print out can be given to the tutor for their information on achievements of their tutees.

Similarly, a print out can be obtained for pupils who ran from each of the Houses for the head of house to see and use. (Figure 9.6).

Figure 9.5
The Tutor Group situation: each pupil can see their position in the Tutor Group as well as their overall position.

```
------------------------------------------------
! YEAR 3 GIRLS CROSS COUNTRY                   !
! HELD ON 26TH OCTOBER                         !
! TUTOR GROUP RESULT FOR 3 BARN                !
------------------------------------------------
!T/G!RACE! NAME                        !TUTOR!
!POS!POS !                             !GROUP!
------------------------------------------------
!1  !1   ! KAREN FRY                   !3BARN!
!2  !7   ! TRACEY HATHAWAY             !3BARN!
!3  !10  ! TINA WEST                   !3BARN!
!4  !15  ! SHARON MIZEN                !3BARN!
------------------------------------------------


------------------------------------------------
! YEAR 3 GIRLS CROSS COUNTRY                   !
! HELD ON 26TH OCTOBER                         !
! TUTOR GROUP RESULT FOR 3 HAR                 !
------------------------------------------------
!T/G!RACE! NAME                        !TUTOR!
!POS!POS !                             !GROUP!
------------------------------------------------
!1  !3   ! CAROLINE FOX                !3HAR !
!2  !5   ! JANE NOTTON                 !3HAR !
!3  !11  ! LISA BEDFORD                !3HAR !
!4  !14  ! LISA HOWARD                 !3HAR !
------------------------------------------------


------------------------------------------------
! YEAR 3 GIRLS CROSS COUNTRY                   !
! HELD ON 26TH OCTOBER                         !
! TUTOR GROUP RESULT FOR 3 HOB                 !
------------------------------------------------
!T/G!RACE! NAME                        !TUTOR!
!POS!POS !                             !GROUP!
------------------------------------------------
!1  !4   ! TRACEY MEACHAM              !3HOB !
!2  !8   ! JULIE HILL                  !3HOB !
!3  !9   ! MANDY OXENHAM               !3HOB !
!4  !12  ! NICOLA GRANGER              !3HOB !
------------------------------------------------


------------------------------------------------
! YEAR 3 GIRLS CROSS COUNTRY                   !
! HELD ON 26TH OCTOBER                         !
! TUTOR GROUP RESULT FOR 3 SKI                 !
------------------------------------------------
!T/G!RACE! NAME                        !TUTOR!
!POS!POS !                             !GROUP!
------------------------------------------------
!1  !2   ! DEBORAH HAWKES              !3SKI !
!2  !6   ! KATHERINE BARNES            !3SKI !
!3  !13  ! LISA WATKINS                !3SKI !
!4  !16  ! TANIA FORD                  !3SKI !
------------------------------------------------
```

```
------------------------------------------------
! YEAR 3 GIRLS CROSS COUNTRY                   !
! HELD ON 26TH OCTOBER                         !
! HOUSE RESULT FOR 3 DUNDRY                    !
------------------------------------------------
!HO !RACE! NAME                        !TUTOR!
!POS!POS !                             !GROUP!
------------------------------------------------
!1  !1   ! KAREN FRY                   !3BARN!
!2  !2   ! DEBORAH HAWKES              !3SKI !
!3  !3   ! CAROLINE FOX                !3HAR !
!4  !5   ! JANE NOTTON                 !3HAR !
!5  !6   ! KATHERINE BARNES            !3SKI !
!6  !8   ! JULIE HILL                  !3HOB !
!7  !9   ! MANDY OXENHAM               !3HOB !
!8  !15  ! SHARON MIZEN                !3BARN!
------------------------------------------------


------------------------------------------------
! YEAR 3 GIRLS CROSS COUNTRY                   !
! HELD ON 26TH OCTOBER                         !
! HOUSE RESULT FOR 3 MENDIP                    !
------------------------------------------------
!HO !RACE! NAME                        !TUTOR!
!POS!POS !                             !GROUP!
------------------------------------------------
!1  !4   ! TRACEY MEACHAM              !3HOB !
!2  !7   ! TRACEY HATHAWAY             !3BARN!
!3  !10  ! TINA WEST                   !3BARN!
!4  !11  ! LISA BEDFORD                !3HAR !
!5  !12  ! NICOLA GRANGER              !3HOB !
!6  !13  ! LISA WATKINS                !3SKI !
!7  !14  ! LISA HOWARD                 !3HAR !
!8  !16  ! TANIA FORD                  !3SKI !
------------------------------------------------
```

Figure 9.6
The House situation: each pupil can see their position in their House as well as their overall position.

The result of the two team competitions forms part of a race summary sheet, the sort of information sheet which the Head needs for reading out in assembly. (Figure 9.7) This sheet shows the runners who finished in the first three places and then the results of the tutor group and house competitions.

Cross Country Race Analysis

```
!-------------------------------------------------!
! YEAR 3 GIRLS CROSS COUNTRY          !
! HELD ON 26TH OCTOBER                !
! RACE SUMMARY                        !
!-------------------------------------------------!
!                                     !
!-------------------------------------------------!
! INDIVIDUAL WINNERS                  !
!-------------------------------------------------!
! RACE  ! NAME               ! TUTOR  !
! POS   !                    ! GROUP  !
!                                     !
! 1     ! KAREN FRY          ! 3BARN  !
! 2     ! DEBORAH HAWKES     ! 3SKI   !
! 3     ! CAROLINE FOX       ! 3HAR   !
!-------------------------------------------------!
!                                     !
!-------------------------------------------------!
! INTER TUTOR GROUP RESULT            !
! BASED ON THE BEST 3 RUNNERS         !
! FROM EACH TUTOR GROUP               !
!-------------------------------------------------!
! POSITION ! TUTOR   ! SCORE          !
!          ! GROUP   !                !
!-------------------------------------------------!
!    1     ! BARN    ! 18 POINTS      !
!-------------------------------------------------!
!    2     ! .HAR    ! 19 POINTS      !
!-------------------------------------------------!
!    3     ! SKI     ! 21 POINTS      !
!-------------------------------------------------!
!    3     ! HOB     ! 21 POINTS      !
!-------------------------------------------------!
!                                     !
!-------------------------------------------------!
! INTER HOUSE RESULT                  !
! BASED ON THE BEST 6 RUNNERS         !
! FROM EACH HOUSE                     !
!-------------------------------------------------!
! POSITION ! HOUSE   ! SCORE          !
!-------------------------------------------------!
!    1     ! DUNDRY  ! 25 POINTS      !
!-------------------------------------------------!
!    2     ! MENDIP  ! 57 POINTS      !
!-------------------------------------------------!
```

Figure 9.7
The Race Summary.

The number of counting runners is determined by the organiser and has to be entered before printing out the race summary. This means a pre-determined number of counting runners can be used or the maximum number according to those running on the day. If there are two houses and there are 55 who finished from one house and 50 from the other then 50 would be the number to count allowing the maximum number of pupils to be used in that result.

All this organisation, preparation and results analysis can be done without ever having to write out one single name. The printed results can be obtained literally within minutes of a race finishing, usually within the time it takes the runners to shower and change.

With most schools now having facilities for photo-copying it is possible to circulate a complete set of all these results very quickly. Alternately, the results could be duplicated using a banda machine. In this case the results can be printed onto a banda skin which is inserted into the computer printer instead of a piece of plain paper before running off the required number of copies on the duplicating machine. This may be a little slower than using a photo-copier but this method would always be available to an event organiser whereas the photo-copier may not be accessible after normal school hours or at weekends.

The second way of organising a cross country event is where all competitors are allocated different runners numbers. This type of organisation is most likely to be adopted for inter school matches, district or county championships or even inter county events although it could be used for an inter house race.

Like before, the names of competitors would have to be known in advance of the event and entered into the Year File program and allocated their race number. School, district or county name replaces the TUTOR GROUP/HOUSE when entering competitors data but as in the previous example all this data about the competitors is then stored on disc.

Recording sheets of a different form can then be produced, figure 9.8, this time to provide space for one person situated at the end of the finishing funnel to enter the number of each runner in the order in which they finish. There would be no need to issue numbered cards at the finish unless the organiser wanted a back-up system for the sake of the runners and team managers.

The computer program for this type of event asks for the runners number and these are fed into the computer as on the recording sheet in the order in which they finished. Each runner is identified on the screen as their number is

CHAPTER 9

AVON SCHOOLS CROSS COUNTRY CHAMPIONSHIPS RECORDING SHEET

DATE : 24th JANUARY ! VENUE : RAINBOW WOODS

AGE GROUP MINOR JUNIOR INTERMEDIATE SENIOR

GENDER BOYS GIRLS

RACE POSITION	RUNNERS NUMBER	RACE POSITION	RUNNERS NUMBER	RACE POSITION	RUNNERS NUMBER
1		17		33	
2		18		34	
3		19		35	
4		20		36	
5		21		37	
6		22		38	
7		23		39	
8		24		40	
9		25		41	
10		26		42	
11		27		43	
12		28		44	
13		29		45	
14		30		46	
15		31		47	
16		32		48	

Figure 9.8
The recording sheet for races where runners are individually numbered (word processed).

entered and checks are made to ensure that the same number is not entered twice. Once all the numbers have been entered, the computer will then produces a print out of the individual result, the team results and a race summary just as before.

This is a very quick method of producing results although more time could be saved if the finish was near enough to an electrical power supply. The computer equipment could then be housed in a tent, caravan or even a mini bus situated at the end of the funnel. Instead of having a person writing down the competitors numbers, the computer can be placed so that the runners numbers are entered directly as they pass. As soon as the last runner has gone through the funnel the results can be printed. As a standby a hand written order could still be obtained after the runners had passed the computer recorder.

Care must be taken with safeguarding any mains power supply which might be taken from a nearby building. Alternately a portable generator could be used to power the computer equipment.

There is no reason why the computer operator has to be the race organiser or even a member of staff. It could be one of those medically excused pupils but preferably it should be carried out by a person with some keyboard experience who can type in numbers accurately and quickly, the former quality more important than the desirable latter.

Some very large cross country or running events, like marathons, could use this latter system but they would need to use a 64K or even a I28K machine to be sure of having enough memory to store and analyse all the data.

Some events are now using bar codes as a means of identifying a runner. These bar codes are part of the runners number attached to their vest which is then read at the end of the race by a light pen connected to the computer. This is one way of using modern technology to enter the runners number into a computer to speed up the race analysis. The results are then processed by the computer as before. This method has been used at the London Marathon but problems have arisen when unofficial runners copied the 'official' race number by adding a 'baked bean tin' bar code. When this happened the computer was thrown by the wrong bar code and caused great confusion and delay by which time the culprits had vanished!

Using bar codes may filter into some school cross country events but hopefully such mis-use should not occur.

THE TRIATHLON

The Triathlon event consists of three activities, swimming, cycling and running. It is an event which is not frequently practiced in schools but it has a large following with adults. There may be more schools events in the future which, when organised, will need computer assistance to work out the results.

Computers are essential due to the complexities of the prolonged start and the need to record the times for the three different activities. Unlike a cross country event, where everyone in the same race starts at the same time, a triathlon has a staggered start due to the limitation of the swimming pool being used. Only a certain number of competitors can safely start their swim together whilst the remainder wait

Cross Country Race Analysis

TRIATHLON 4th MAY		RACE DATA IN FINAL POSITION ORDER								
(Times indicated are HOURS, MINUTES and SECONDS AFTER 10.00 a.m.)										
(A = Avon competitor : V = Veteran : F = Female : TM = Team Number)										
POS	(NUM)	NAME		A	V	F	TM	START	END SWIM	END CYCLE	END RUN	TOTAL
1	(119)	ALBERT	SMITH				40	01.20.13	01.26.49	02.32.00	03.05.20	01.45.07
2	(342)	DAVIS	HARRIS		V			00.16.25	00.23.17	01.30.00	02.02.56	01.46.31
3	(440)	GEORGE	COLEMAN	A				02.23.33	02.28.36	03.34.00	04.10.14	01.46.41
4	(363)	ALAN	READ					01.12.58	01.19.16	02.25.00	03.00.49	01.47.51
5	(433)	HENRY	FROST	A	V		32	00.24.41	00.30.23	01.38.00	02.13.03	01.48.22

Figure 9.9
The type of detailed results required at the end of a Triathlon event.

until called.

Recordings are made for each competitor at the beginning and end of their swim, at the end of their cycle and at the end of their run. The total time taken can then be worked out as can their individual activity times.

For a large entry of 400 or 500 competitors the amount of data to be collected, stored, analysed and printed out is considerable. By hand it could prove to be too much but the computer will produce the winner shortly after the last person has completed the course.

Like the cross country events all competitors names and numbers have to be entered before race day. The competitors number is entered into the computer before inserting that persons time for one of the three activities. Once all times have been entered the computer will work out the total elapsed time.

When a check of the positions is required the computer will sort out the elapsed times, put them in order and display the findings. (Figure 9.9).

ORIENTEERING

The analysis and presentation of results in the sport of orienteering would benefit considerably by the use of a computer. The major problem for this sport lies in the remote venues, usually in forests, well away from mains electricity. If the power can be obtained by using a portable generator, or a portable computer or by moving the start/finish area to a more convenient location, then the computer can ease the pressure of work on the day for the event organiser.

Like the triathlon, many orienteering events have a prolonged start. Unlike the triathlon, there are likely to be several different courses being run at the same time. Although a very effective card system is operated, it could be made more efficient with the aid of the computer, especially for producing and printing out the final results after the last competitor has finished.

The computer would log out each competitor noting their name, course and time of departure. On their return the difference in time will be calculated and saved. At the end, these times will be sorted and printed out on paper according to the different catagory of race. The program will allow for those who retire or those who miss or find the wrong control. A 'human' check on each control card will have to be made to verify that each competitor has completed the course.

Many orienteering competitions are held over a series of events with points being awarded according to positions,. This 'league' type of competition could be easily handled on a computer producing up to date points and positions very quickly after each event.

GENERAL

When dealing with big events it is essential to get entries in early to give the organiser time to enter the competitors details into the computer. Once that has been carried out then no further writing of names is done. One large club event has about 1500 entries for their big race of the year. The organiser used to take three days off work to allocate each competitor with a number and put the entries into alphabetical order. This is now done on the computer and the club are getting lists printed of competitors in race number order, alphabetical order and club order. It only takes a minute or so to complete one of these sorts and the lists are being used as the basis for the event programme.

There is nothing worse for the organiser at the end of a race than to face the prospect of having to wade through piles of papers and figures to work out the result and get them printed. The computer will carry out both of these operations and so any event organiser can now go home afterwards with the analysis completed. There may still be some further adminstration, such as circulating people with the details of the result but most of the pressure will be taken off the event organiser on the day by using the computer.

Cross Country Race Analysis

Fixtures, Competition and Results

Competition is an important aspect of physical education which will involve the organising P.E. teacher in a fair amount of administration. Some events will be bigger and more important than others but essentially they all involve advanced planning, the recording of scores and the analysis and circulation of the results.

Some of this, as seen earlier, can be carried out effectively and more efficiently by using a computer. Other competitive activities can also benefit by using a computer before, during and after an event.

FIXTURES – LEAGUES

It can be a daunting task for those who are prepared to be responsible for organising school sports leagues to have to make the draw for the order of matches, to record all the results as the season progresses and keep an up-to-date league table. The computer can remove the worry of all this administration with the aid of a league computer program.

The program could offer the option to play fixtures at home and away or just a single game. If a game has to be played every week, the day and date can be programmed in, avoiding specified dates, like holidays. The computer will then generate a full fixture list based upon a random draw. As the season progresses results are fed into the program at any time. A check on the points and positions within the league can be printed out in the form of a league table whenever the organiser requires this.

This system could be used for an inter school, an inter house or inter tutor group competition. For a Netball League the fixtures would be as shown in figure 10.1. The league has six teams,

```
NETBALL FIXTURES
    TUESDAY - 20 - JANUARY - 87
        ORANGE V RED
        BLUE V WHITE
        GREEN V YELLOW
    TUESDAY - 27 - JANUARY - 87
        YELLOW V BLUE
        GREEN V ORANGE
        RED V WHITE
    TUESDAY - 3 - FEBRUARY - 87
        WHITE V GREEN
        RED V BLUE
        YELLOW V ORANGE
    TUESDAY - 10 - FEBRUARY - 87
        RED V GREEN
        BLUE V ORANGE
        WHITE V YELLOW
    TUESDAY - 17 - FEBRUARY - 87
        YELLOW V RED
        GREEN V BLUE
        ORANGE V WHITE
    TUESDAY - 3 - MARCH - 87
        BLUE V RED
        GREEN V WHITE
        ORANGE V YELLOW
    TUESDAY - 10 - MARCH - 87
        GREEN V RED
        ORANGE V BLUE
        YELLOW V WHITE
    TUESDAY - 17 - MARCH - 87
        WHITE V RED
        ORANGE V GREEN
        BLUE V YELLOW
    TUESDAY - 24 - MARCH - 87
        YELLOW V GREEN
        WHITE V BLUE
        RED V ORANGE
    TUESDAY - 31 - MARCH - 87
        BLUE V GREEN
        WHITE V ORANGE
        RED V YELLOW
```

Figure 10.1
Spring Term Netball fixtures generated by the computer.

Fixtures, Competition and Results

playing matches both at home and away against every opponent. They are to play every Tuesday, except during the Half Term holiday week.

Half-way through the fixture list the league positions showing full details of points looks like figure 10.2. All of this can be created and printed

TEAMS	HOME					AWAY					PTS
	PD	W	D	L	F	A	W	D	L	F	A	PTS
RED	5	2	1	0	23	20	2	0	0	14	9	14
BLUE	5	3	0	0	20	10	0	1	1	16	17	12
YELLOW	5	2	0	0	16	10	0	1	2	12	16	10
ORANGE	5	1	1	0	14	12	0	1	2	16	20	9
GREEN	5	0	1	1	7	11	1	0	2	12	15	8
WHITE	5	1	0	2	13	14	0	0	2	7	16	7

Figure 10.2
The Netball league positions at Half Term.

out by the computer within minutes, saving the organiser a great deal of time.

FIXTURES – KNOCK OUT

Some sports have their competition based on the knock out principle. As before the computer can make all the draws, record the winners and display the games for the following round.

Twelve players have entered for a Badminton competition. The computer could run this competition in two ways. Firstly, after entering the names of the competitors, the computer would make a random draw to select those players who have to play a preliminary match and those who receive a first round bye. Once the results have been entered, the computer would make a new draw for the subsequent rounds to the final. (Figure 10.3).

The other way a computer can organise a knock out competition is to pair successive winners until the finals are reached as shown in figure 10.4. The operations to run this computer program are the same as before and even the outcomes may turn out to be the same.

Either way these computer programs will help to ease the administrative pressures during a competition for the event organiser.

```
The fixtures this round are...

    KATE HOLLAND  v  BYE

    ALISON PINK  v  BYE

    JOAN SMITH  v  BYE

  FRANCIS JONES  v  BYE


      LIZ SLEEP  v  SUSAN HARRISON

    DEBBIE GILL  v  HELEN HOPE

 WENDY WALLACE  v  SARAH GREEN

    CHRIS WEST  v  TRACEY BROWN

        QUARTER FINALS

      LIZ SLEEP  v  HELEN HOPE

    ALISON PINK  v  CHRIS WEST

  FRANCIS JONES  v  KATE HOLLAND

    JOAN SMITH  v  WENDY WALLACE

         SEMI-FINALS

    CHRIS WEST  v  JOAN SMITH

    HELEN HOPE  v  KATE HOLLAND

          THE FINAL

    JOAN SMITH  v  KATE HOLLAND
```

Figure 10.3
A knock out Badminton competition – each round has a random draw.

```
              BADMINTON COMPETITION


  Preliminary Round      Quarter Final        Semi-Final           FINAL

  Joan Smith      ) 15
  Chris West      ) 9     Joan Smith    ) 15

  Sarah Green     ) 11    Helen Hope    ) 10    Joan Smith    ) 15
  Helen Hope      ) 15

  Liz Sleep       ) 15
  Kate Holland    ) 8     Liz Sleep     ) 9     Francis Jones ) 12    Joan Smith    ) 13

  Debbie Gill     ) 10    Francis Jones ) 15
  Francis Jones   ) 15

  Susan Harrison  )
  Bye             )       Susan Harrison ) 15

  Tracey Brown    )       Tracey Brown   ) 12   Susan Harrison ) 9    Wendy Wallace ) 15
  Bye             )

  Wendy Wallace   )
  Bye             )       Wendy Wallace  ) 15   Wendy Wallace  ) 15

  Alison Pink     )       Alison Pink    ) 13
  Bye             )
```

Figure 10.4
The same Badminton Competition with the more normal knock out procedure of pairing winners.

WEIGHT LIFTING

A school boy weight lifting competition is purely a number crunching exercise when it comes to working out the results. A simple computer program would ease considerably the pressures on the officials at the time of the competition.

There will be boys of different ages and weights competing against each other but there is a formulae to balance out these differences, $((100 - \text{Body Weight in Kg}) \times 2)$. Competitors have three opportunities to lift as much as possible in two different methods of lifting, the snatch and the clean and jerk.

The final result is based on the figure produced

Picture 10.1

Fixtures, Competition and Results

by the formulae plus the sum of the highest weight achieved in each lift. Officials first enter into the computer program all competitors names and their body weights. (Figure 10.5)

```
WEIGHT LIFTING COMPETITION

COMPETITORS NUMBER   :


COMPETITORS NAME     :


SCHOOL / CLUB        :


BODY WEIGHT          :


STARTING WEIGHTS

SNATCH               :


CLEAN and JERK       :
```

Figure 10.5
Entry requirements to be fed into the computer before the start of a weight lifting competition.

Officials will want to know the weight that each competitor is to attempt first in each method of lifting. The computer can then display the order of lifting according to the weight on the bar. The best lift achieved in the snatch is displayed and stored whilst the clean and jerk takes place.

During the clean and jerk, it would help competitors to know how much they have to lift to win the competition, or at least to beat those who have already finished. The computer can calculate the competitors current total and compare that with the best of those who have already finished and display that difference. This difference will be the weight that the competitor has to lift to take the lead. (Figure 10.6) These calculations would be displayed on the computer monitor of the event official but there should also be a second monitor placed in the warm up room for competitors to see the up-to-date position of the competition as it progresses.

As competitors finish their last lift the computer can work out immediately the final total for that person, compare that figure with all others who have finished and put them all into rank order. (Figure 10.7).

As soon as the last competitor has had his final lift the result is displayed, it can b sent to the printer, photocopied and be available to competitors on paper within minutes.

GYMNASTICS

Here is another sport which lends itself to computerisation. Although the numerical calculation may not be particularly difficult it is often the 'pressure' placed on officials during the actual running of the event which can cause mistakes to be made. Providing the correct scores are entered initially, the computer can be relied upon to carry out the correct calculations.

A school gymnastics competition may consist of just one or two exercises instead of the normal six for men, or four for women. No matter how many exercises form the basis of the competition the scoring is the same. Each competitor is given a mark out of ten by each of four judges. The highest and the lowest marks are eliminated leaving the two intermediate scores to be averaged. This is the mark given to the competitor.

A gymnastics computer program will need all the competitors names and their schools/clubs, just like the weight lifting program. These are entered before the competition starts. For every exercise the competitor is identified and the four scores entered into the computer. The program will automatically ignore the top and bottom mark whilst averaging out the other two marks and displaying them immediately on screen.

All the scores for each individual are saved so that team scores and positions can be determined. Such a program would be essential for an inter school or county gymnastics championship but a more simple version would suffice for a small competition within school. For this, again names are entered first and then scores are given by one judge. Points are awarded for two events and the totals and positions calculated at the end of the competition.

ATHLETICS – FIVE STAR AWARD SCHEME

In essence the conception of the Five Star

```
WEIGHT LIFTING COMPETITION

COMPETITORS NUMBER    :   12

COMPETITORS NAME      :   JOHN SMITH

SCHOOL / CLUB         :   THE MARY ROSE SCHOOL

BODY WEIGHT (Kg)      :   53.4

SNATCH
                    LIFT 1          :   27.5
                    LIFT 2          :   32.5
                    LIFT 3          :   35.0          BEST LIFT :  35.0

CLEAN and JERK

WEIGHT NEEDED TO TAKE LEAD :   62.5
                    LIFT 1          :   50.0
WEIGHT NEEDED TO TAKE LEAD :   62.5
                    LIFT 2          :   60.0
WEIGHT NEEDED TO TAKE LEAD :   62.5
                    LIFT 3          :   XXXX          BEST LIFT :  60.0

                                 TOTAL LIFTED              :  95.0

                                 TOTAL SCORE               :  188.2

                                 CURRENT POSITION          :  2

                                 CURRENT LEADER  SIMON HALL  :  188.4
```

Figure 10.6
A competitor's computerised "score card" after his last lift.

Award Scheme is very simple. Pupils gain points according to performance and the total score achieved in certain events will indicate the grade to be awarded. However, the task is compounded by the different age groups and the many different events. The tables, whilst clear, have to be consulted to check every pupil performance. The administrative task can be enormous if the award is being taken by all pupils in a large school as names, performances and points have to be constantly written down, amended and added up.

Computer programs have been written to try to ease the administration of this award. Pupils names are entered and events listed before details of performances can be inserted. Lists are then produced indicating the awards achieved.

It is till a lengthy task to set up and operate this program, so the teacher will have to assess whether it is better to continue with the administration by hand rather than by computer.

```
WEIGHT LIFTING COMPETITION

CURRENT POSITION

   1      SIMON HALL         188.4
   2      JOHN SMITH         188.2
   3      DAVID GREEN        183.6
   4      JEREMY HILL        175.3
   5      GRAHAM GOLDING     170.5
```

Figure 10.7
Competitors and spectators can be given a regular up dating of the positions of lifters who have already finished in the competition.

Fixtures, Competition and Results

CRICKET

Here is a sport which handles a vast and constant amount of numerical data. Television coverage of important games are constantly displaying interesting facts about run rates, average runs per over required or bowling figures. Such figures would be difficult to obtain at regular intervals from a hand written cricket score book. Such figures can only be obtained so quickly by using a computer.

It is unlikely that such a sophisticated program is a necessity for every school cricket match but there is no reason why a computerised cricket scoring program should not be used in schools. There might be a problem of providing a safe power supply to the edge of the field although schools which have a scorebox or pavillion may have power there already.

BASKETBALL

Basketball has been receiving more coverage on television and as a result there has been a need to analyse and display facts about the game, as in cricket.

As well as maintaining the score as the game goes on, analysis can take place of certain key aspect of the game. Throughout the game a record can be kept of the following –

Shots and layups taken.
Shots and layups scored.
Free throws taken.
Free throws scored.
Offensive rebounds taken.
Defensive rebounds taken.
Steals.
Losses.
Assists.
Blocks.
Foul counts.

From this data a detailed analysis is possible for each team to study their strengths and weaknesses after the game. Each player would have listed a detailed analysis of their contribution to the game and would soon see where their highest and lowest percentages of shots had been achieved. This information would help in the planning of future training programmes, to enable the coach to concentrate on areas of weakness shown up by individuals or the team as a whole. If figures are obtained from other fixtures then a team can plan their match strategy against particular opponents.

The program would also supply the audience with a more informed appreciation of the game and the relative merits of each team.

Not all of these features may be deemed necessary for school matches but for important county school fixtures it may be worth considering.

AMERICAN FOOTBALL

The Americans of course require every fact and feature displayed immediately about their games. Now that American Football is being shown in this country those facts are being brought to our screens as well.

There is a lot to be learnt from this principle of game analysis as it occurs. Like the basketball, it is only possible with the aid of a computer. There is more to using a computer during games than just displaying the immediate score. The Americans store all their facts about each game as a season progresses so that facts are available or any game or over all the games that have occured.

OTHERS

It is unlikely that outdoor games such as football, rugby, hockey, netball, rounders, etc., will use computers to display their scores. However, there is a place for schools to establish programs which will collect and store factual information about each game. Date of game, opponents, result and who scored could be stored for analysis. At any time during the season the computer could provide a quick summary of these facts.

The game analysis programs do have a relevance for the study of styles of play. These should be seriously considered for use in school competitions. Some pupils who may not be the talented games players may have an important role to play here in being the operators of such systems whilst a game is taking place.

SCOREBOARD

Computers can be used as a scoreboard for some 'low' scoring games indoors by using a large monitor to diplay the score. Big numbers, taking up the whole screen, could be shown for say a volleyball match. This would only be appropriate to indoor activities although care should be taken in the swimming pool. Here the computer would have to be very well protected from getting wet or damp and the safety of the wiring would have to be an important consideration.

Ideas for such scoring and analysis programs can be obtained from a variety of sources. Some computer publications, books or magazines, from time to time will publish programs which can be adapted to act as scoreboards or game analysis programs.

Fixtures, Competition and Results

Computers as a Teaching Aid

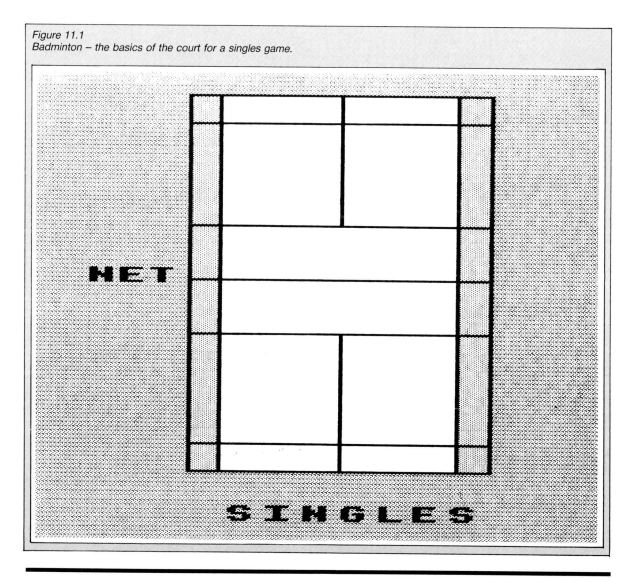

Figure 11.1
Badminton – the basics of the court for a singles game.

Computers as a Teaching Aid

Physical education is by no means a totally practical subject and there are times when it is better to teach certain aspects of an activity in a 'theory' session. Various techniques may be used, such as chalk and talk, slides, films or videos. Another alternative is to use the computer as the means of displaying factual material through the use of grahics material, sound and text.

Children do seem to retain facts when they are presented on the television and the power of this medium must not be under-estimated. Better retention of these facts may result from seeing certain information about sport displayed on a television or on computer monitor.

Computer assisted learning programs could provide the P.E. teacher with a colourful and exciting factual introduction to any new activity in the physical education curriculum. Whilst posters, drawings or worksheets can provide the same information, the computer has the advantage of being able to make things move, it has colour, sound and other visual effects likely to appeal more to children.

Some of the more simple facts about sports can be easily presented via a computer by using one of the many 'painting' or picture type programs now on the market.

Our Sports Hall floors are often covered in a mass of lines for many different games and trying to explain which lines are which can be very confusing at the best of times, particularly to less able pupils. Drawing out these lines and explaining their function with a few words can be achieved very quickly on the computer using these picture programs. (Figure 11.1).

A page, or more precisely, a screen full of text can be created in the same colourful way that Ceefax and Oracle display their information. Like the painting programs it is easy and quick to use a 'teletext' program.

For the game of badminton the computer can be set up to run a sequence of screens consisting of some pictures and some text. The pictures could show and name the lines, display the differences in the size of court for singles and doubles or go on to show the respective service and receiving areas. (Figures 11.2 and 11.3). Following each picture there could be one or two 'pages' of text explaining in more detail the significance of the pictures in relation to the actual rules of the game.

Such a 'teaching aid' could be produced in two ways. Firstly, in an automatic mode whereby sufficient time would be allowed for viewing and reading before the next page appeared on the computer monitor. Alternately, the pages could be moved on by the user who might be the teacher, giving a class lesson with the aid of the computer, or by a pupil, or pupils, who might be working through the sequence as a 'work sheet' at their own rate.

In either case the generous use of colour, when the program is being made, will enhance the appearance of such pictures making the most important aspects stand out very clearly.

The picture programs can also be used to help illustrate other material produced by the P.E. department. The Faculty Handbook, the Sports Day programme or the Cross Country Results could all benefit by some artistic assistance. (Figures 11.4, 11.5 and 11.6).

GRAPHICS

A computer can be directly programmed to plot certain lines to produce certain predetermined shapes. These shapes could be human figures performing certain 'skills' in an ideal manner. If several of these are linked together with only a short time interval between each 'picture' then the figure can be made to appear to move.

A static picture of the sequence can be made using the earlier painting program (figure 11.7) but when these individual figures are made much larger and superimposed on top of each other then animation can be created. The time interval between each diagram can be regulated by the user so a teacher could explain particular points about each figure or run the whole series to give apparent movement, either at a slow or fast speed.

COMPUTER GAMES

Visit any high street shop selling computers and there will be rows and rows of computer games. Unfortunately they have little to do with the sorts of 'games' with which physical education is associated. They are mainly of the 'zap' and 'pow' space variety although some are

Figure 11.2
Badminton service areas for singles.

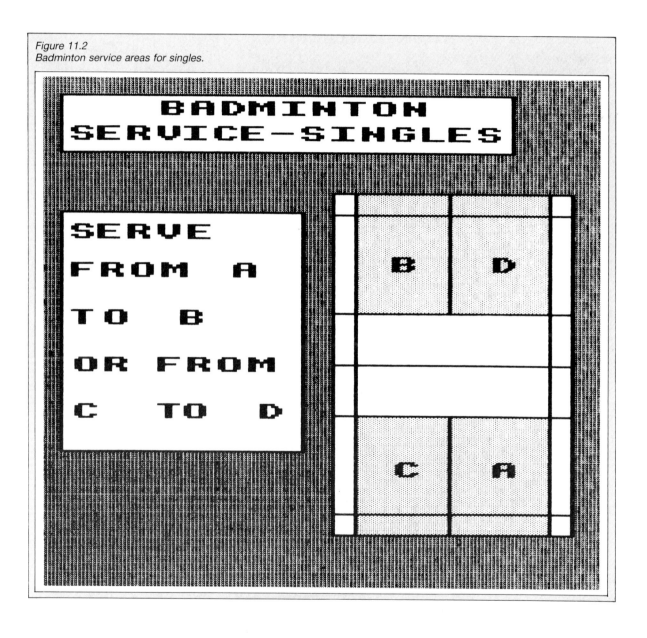

Figure 11.3
Badminton service areas for doubles.

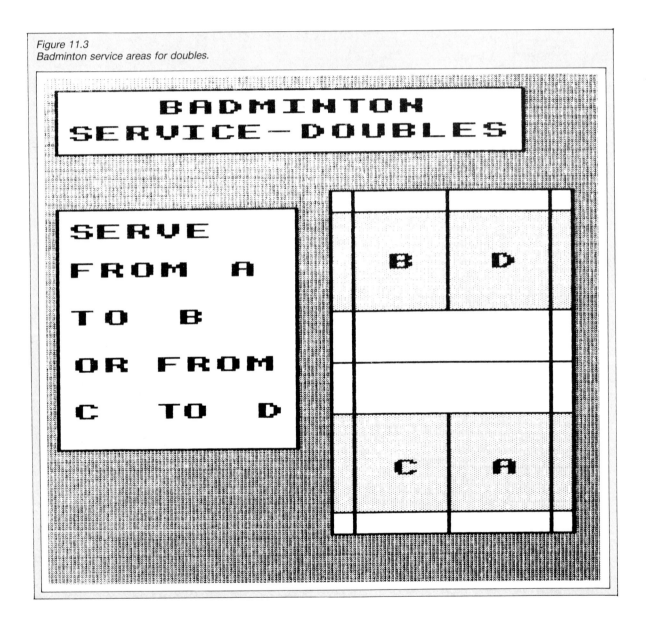

Figure 11.4
Computer generated front cover for the P.E. Departments' documents.

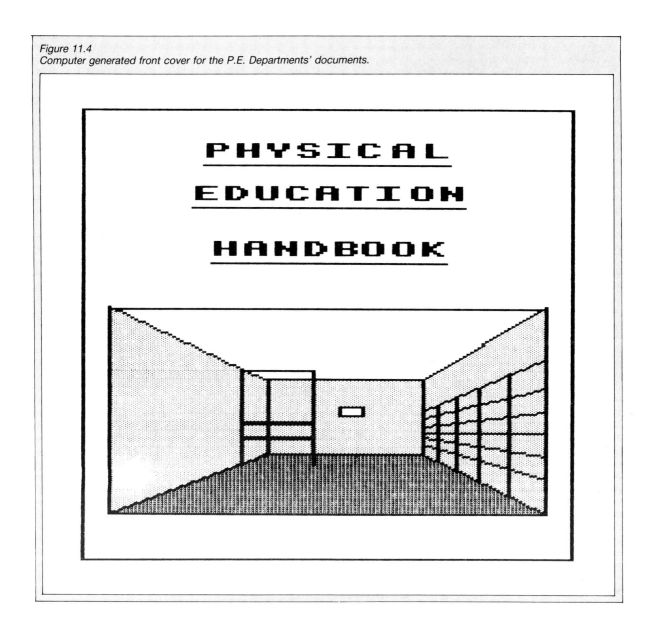

Computers as a Teaching Aid

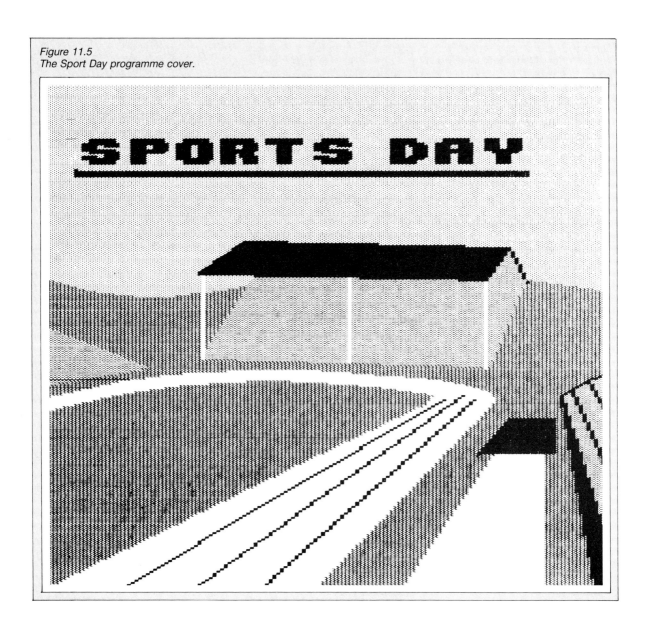

Figure 11.5
The Sport Day programme cover.

Figure 11.6
The cross country programme or results cover.

Computers as a Teaching Aid

Figure 11.7
Graphics programs can be made to illustrate technique.

more down to earth adventure games.

It is rare that a computer version of a sporting game appears in the shops, especially for the BBC. When they do they are often very disappointing. Games such as the athletics one portraying the decathlon event are more a test of the destructability of the computer than anything else since the user has to hit various keys as fast as possible to achieve running speed. Apart from learning which activities are part of a decathlon competition there is little opportunity to increase knowledge or skill in any of the decathlon events.

In some of the football simulation games it is the computer which 'plays' the games and the user has little or no control over the outcomes. Simulation games such as managing a football club involves buying and selling players, selecting a team and seeing what the computer will present in the way of results over a 'football season'. This can be an interesting game for youngsters to try their hand at 'management' and is perhaps one of the few games where pupils can learn something relating to a real game situation.

Very rarely will a computer game provide the user with a real learning situation. Cricket is a game where many decisions have to be constantly taken by both the batting and fielding sides. With two pupils 'playing' a game of computer cricket and being responsible for the opposing sides, one can make the decisions on how best to set out the fielders and to select the pace of the bowler whilst the other takes the batting decisions.

The computer presents two views of the pitch, a plan and a side elevation. As the bowler runs in and bowls the action is frozen at the point where the ball makes contact with the ground. The person acting as 'batsman' now has to decide which of nine different batting strokes to play. Knowledge of the pace and direction of the ball along with an ability to select the correct stroke has to be taken into account for each ball.

This is where good teaching can be carried out by debating the merits of each shot. The pupils would need to know when it is appropriate to use each of the nine batting shots available to them. These are:

Hook
Cut
On Drive
Off Drive
Straight Drive
Leg Glance
Back Defence
Forward Defence
No Shot

Scoreboards can be displayed to inform the users of the state of play. Such a program could, on a wet day, provide the P.E. teacher with a relevant lesson on batting strokes and field placing whilst at the same time 'playing' a game of cricket.

There is a vast potential for computer programs to be used as a teaching aid in physical education. Regretably there are so few of any real quality. Some have excellent graphics where tennis balls are shown in such fine detail moving across a three dimensional court that even the shadow from the 'sun' can be seen moving across the floor! Some programs have very good ideas but have poor quality graphics.

Perhaps one day, compact interactive laser discs will be used in P.E. departments to assist with the teaching of any major or minor sporting activity. Is this too much to hope for? The possibility is real enough as the technology is already available and being used today.

The interactive video disc is a solid disc which is scanned by lasers and controlled by computers. The discs can hold a vast amount of data, seven and a half million words, sound and many picures all of a high quality. The Doomsday project disc holds data and pictures of the whole of the country and details about any village which the user requests can be displayed within seconds.

This laser disc technology could be of enormous benefit to physical education. A disc could be a reservoir of useful information being able to display details such as the results, teams, venues and rules of any sporting activity. However, it could have a more important function, that of a teaching aid.

How often have P.E. teachers tried to explain, on a blackboard, magnetised board or even on the field of play, how a flowing passing, attacking move can be made. Similarly, defensive moves need to be studied and understood. The laser

Computers as a Teaching Aid

disc could provide the opportunity to examine various alternative strategies of play and compare their effectiveness.

In time our computers may be linked as much to compact discs as to disc drives and printers. The use of interactive video discs, fibre optics, nuclear magnetic resonance and computer enhanced imaging is being used to make a 'voyage' through the body for medical students. There is no reason why this technology should not be applied for physical education purposes.

There are computer programs which have been written primarily for other subjects which have cross curricular links with physical education, particularly science related programs. There are a number of different programs which test the users REACTIONS. Three different types of test are available, one to test reaction to 'light' or vision, a second to test reaction to noise and a third to test the reaction to a situation where only one response is acceptable given a variety of circumstances.

The vision tests may have anything suddenly appearing on the screen from faces to shapes or even a new colour and the user has to 'hit' a key as soon as it appears. Usually a number of attempts are given and an average time displayed at the end. Some of these programs are fun to use although some pupils need to be restrained from hitting the computer keys too hard. The relevance of such programs can be discussed with pupils and a study made of which games need quick reactions. Those pupils who achieve good times might be better at some sports than those with slower times.

Similarly, the test where the user has to react to a computer generated noise could have a bearing on certain sports. The third and more complicated test where the user has to react to only one of many different situations requires a higher level of attention. Anyone failing to apply themselves to this task will perform badly. If there are many pupils around the computer for this test then extra 'pressure' is put on the user giving them a very real measure of their level of concentration.

Another program associated with vision explains the nature of the 'blind spot' and how it comes about. Using the computer the user can locate and measure the size of their own blind spot. Such a program would need to be used as part of a teacher led discussion on the importance and problems of vision in sporting activities.

DIET is another aspect which can be related to physical education. There are several programs available to analyse the amount and type of food being eaten depending on sex and age. They will display the 'ideal' diet for a particular person in terms of protein, fat, carbohydrate, fibre, energy, calcium, iron, vitamin C and vitamin B1. The user has to enter their daily food intake which is compared with the suggestions made by the computer. Analysis can be made of the composition of a diet as to whether it contains a balance of nutrients.

Hypothetical diets could be inserted to see what excesses or deficiencies may occur. The diet of top class sports persons in different sports could be analysed to compare the energy needs of different activities. The use of such a program would have to be accompanied by the teacher explaining the role and nature of nutrients and what constitutes a healthy, balanced diet.

There are now quick ways of measuring the actual fat content of the body with a portable computer. Instead of submerging people totally in water, the device measures the electrical resistance of the body to calculate and print out the quantity of fat, lean tissue and body water.

For any computer program to be a worthwhile teaching aid it must be of good quality, an interesting stimulant and informative. If it involves the pupil directly at the computer it should also be fun to operate and easy to follow. If the computer is used in lesson time as a teaching aid then pupil learning must take place, otherwise the program should be saved for extra-curricular time or for use at home. The P.E. teacher has to ask himself whether he can teach a topic better with the help of a particular computer program. If the answer is yes, then it should be used; if not, then the topic should be well taught without the aid of the computer.

Reports and Pupil Profiles

The majority of the time devoted to completing pupil reports should be spent on writing relevant comments and not on the mundane tasks of putting in names, tutor group, house, subject, date, teacher's name, teaching group, etc.

Little wonder that having entered all that basic information about each pupil that the teacher becomes reluctant to make a very detailed and worthwhile comment. This is where the computer can relieve the teacher of many of these simple but time consuming tasks.

If all the names and details of every pupil have already been written into a Year File program (Chapter 4) and stored on disc, then that data can be incorporated into a physical education report form BEFORE they are given to the teachers to write. In this way the teacher has got more time to devote to the writing and hopefully more detailed and constructive comments will be forthcoming.

There are many ways of setting up such a system of computerised reports but first the whole issue of report writing and pupil profiling has to be discussed as an issue across the whole school and across the whole curriculum. Once agreement has been reached on the format then suitable programs can be written which will link into the stored pupil data file.

Two examples will be examined here, one which looks at the printing of named reports for the P.E. department whilst the other will examine a system of building up a set of pupil reports into a five year pupil profile.

PUPIL REPORTS

Every school will want a slightly different format for their school reports. Anyone with a little computer programming experience could easily design and write their own departmental version. The size of the report is critical and must be agreed in the early stages of planning. The size will determie just how much detail can be included on the report.

The size has to be linked to the use of fan-fold paper. This is paper which is continuous but has perforations every 28 cms (just less than A4 size) and so this length will affect the number of reports which can be printed on each page. Realistically, the maximum on one sheet will be three reports but they will be brief and narrow. Two reports, each about A5 in size, will be the more popular option. Some schools may even prefer the larger space and opt for the full page.

The design of a school report requires much careful thought as to what it should contain and where such information should be placed. In constructing one such report, of an A5 size, it can be seen that some information will be common to all reports, such as the school name, the Year group and the subject. In addition there would be all the headings or titles for the various sections. These items would all need to be built into the program as constants. (Figure 12.1).

There will be a number of variables which will include the pupil name and tutor group. These pieces of data are available from the Year File program and they can easily be inserted into their correct place on the report thereby eliminating the need for staff to write out any names.

The design of the comment area becomes very individual to each department. The design could be very simple, leaving all the remaining space for a written general comment.

Reports and Pupil Profiles

```
-------------------------------------------------------------------------------
 THE MARY ROSE SCHOOL      NAME          JOHN  SMITH
 SUBJECT REPORT            TUTOR GROUP    1  HAR
 YEAR 1                    SUBJECT        PHYSICAL  EDUCATION
 DATE                      TEACHER
-------------------------------------------------------------------------------

 GENERAL COMMENT:




                      SIGNED .....................
-------------------------------------------------------------------------------
```

Figure 12.1
A simple P.E. report printed and named by the computer.

Alternately, each subject could use some of that space to incorporate an assessment of specific aspects of school work. To streamline the writing task a system of ticking one of four grades might be adopted. (Figure 12.2).

In physical education it might be decided to include comments on the pupils general level of effort, their level of participation, their attitude, co-operation with others, their level of fitness and their level of ability in certain activities. In addition there should still be an opportunity to make a general comment before the report is signed by the teacher.

Once the format and design of this type of report has been agreed, the relevant headings have to be written into a computer program. The program will access the data in the Year File and insert the details of each pupil to construct a personalised P.E. report. To printout a whole year group may take half an hour or an hour depending on the numbers in the Year. The computer can be set up to run this program at the beginning of a lesson and then left to get on with the printing. At the end of the lesson all the P.E. reports will be printed, named and awaiting their comments.

PUPIL PROFILING

The report is a single document, the profile is a record or picture of many such reports. The production of the second P.E. report, described earlier, needs to be modified if it is to fulfill the profile requirements. In this profiling example, there are two main differences. First, the profile program is based upon a bank of written comments created in an assessment grid rather than the system of ticking one of four possible grades. Secondly, use is made of the computer's ability to store each pupil's comments so that they can be added to and recalled over a number of years.

To set up this program the P.E. department has to work out the nature of the headings or areas of work on which they wish to comment. These headings could be a mixture between comments of a more general and educational nature and those which would be specific activity based comments. For each heading five short, written comments have to be created ranging from very good to very poor with a sixth being a 'no comment'. (Figure 12.3) The latter is for those times when pupils may not have done one of the activities or for those occasions when

```
----------------------------------------------------------------------------
THE MARY ROSE SCHOOL      NAME       JOHN  SMITH
SUBJECT REPORT            TUTOR GROUP  1  HAR
YEAR 1                    SUBJECT     PHYSICAL  EDUCATION
DATE                      TEACHER
----------------------------------------------------------------------------

EFFORT                    Unsatisfactory - Satisfactory - Good - Very Good

PARTICIPATION             Unsatisfactory - Satisfactory - Good - Very Good

ATTITUDE                  Unsatisfactory - Satisfactory - Good - Very Good

CO-OPERATION WITH OTHERS  Unsatisfactory - Satisfactory - Good - Very Good

LEVEL OF FITNESS          Unsatisfactory - Satisfactory - Good - Very Good

ABILITY IN THESE ACTIVITIES

GYMNASTICS                Unsatisfactory - Satisfactory - Good - Very Good

SWIMMING                  Unsatisfactory - Satisfactory - Good - Very Good

HOCKEY                    Unsatisfactory - Satisfactory - Good - Very Good

GENERAL COMMENT:



                SIGNED .....................

----------------------------------------------------------------------------
```

Figure 12.2
A more detailed P.E. report, again printed and named by the computer.

Figure 12.3
Part of the pupil assessment grid.

PROFILE ASSESSMENT GRID						
HEADING	1	2	3	4	5	6
EFFORT	always works very hard	works hard	works well	could try harder	shows little effort	no comment
PARTICIPATION	fully participates in each lesson	etc.	etc.			
ATTITUDE	etc.					
etc.						

Reports and Pupil Profiles

a comment would be inappropriate.

The comments in this grid need not all be short descriptive phrases but they could be a 'mark' such as GRADE 1, GRADE 2, etc., or even a 'grade' such as A, B, C, D, and E. Deciding each phrase or the criteria for awarding a Grade 2 or a B will take much time to resolve. The grid in figure 12.3 is only the start of what could be a large structure of 10 or 12 headings, each with their respective comments.

The earlier report program was a means of printing out a mass of reports, all 'topped and tailed', which the teacher filled in later. There are two ways of 'writing' the report profiles. Each teacher can sit at a computer to 'write' and print out all their reports selecting the most appropriate comment for each heading for each pupil.

```
JOHN  SMITH  of  1  HAR

EFFORT

1. always works very hard

2. works hard

3. works well

4. could try harder

5. shows little effort

6. no comment. Go to next heading

SELECT NUMBER REQUIRED
```

Figure 12.4
The comments for each heading are displayed on the computer monitor in this way. The teacher selects a comment by pressing the appropriate numbers.

```
--------------------------------------------------------------------------
THE MARY ROSE SCHOOL       PHYSICAL   EDUCATION   REPORT

Date : December 1986       JOHN  SMITH

Taught by : Mr Jones       1  HAR
--------------------------------------------------------------------------
EFFORT                     John always works very hard

PARTICIPATION              John fully participates in each lesson

ATTITUDE                   John has a very positive attitude towards physical
                           education

CO-OPERATION WITH OTHERS   John sometimes has difficulty when working in a
                           group

LEVEL OF FITNESS           John is an extemely fit pupil

IN GYMNASTICS              John has a good level of body control

IN SWIMMING                John has achieved a grade 2 standard

IN HOCKEY                  John is grade C

GENERAL COMMENT :
```

A very promising and positive start. Well done

Signed .. *A. Jones.* ....

Figure 12.5
The printed P.E. report based on written comments.

This could prove a problem in a school with a lot of staff and access to only a limited number of computers. If agreement was possible, office staff might be able to enter the data from report proformas filled in by the individual teachers but based on this system.

As before, the basic data about each pupil is obtained from the Year File whilst details about the date, Year, subject and teachers name can be inserted into the program at the time it is used.

Pupils are identified by their reference numbers and once selected their name appears with the first of the headings. (Figure 12.4) The six comments are displayed for that heading and the teacher selects the appropriate one. Once all the headings and comments have appeared then the report can be printed out. (Figure 12.5).

At the end of 'writing' a set of reports for pupils in Year 1 the data is then saved. This is done in a numerical way so that for instance, the third comment for the fourth heading,"co-operation with others – sometimes has difficulty when working in a group" – would be saved as a 3. The numerical equivalent of the comment can be displayed for each pupil for year 1. (Figure 12.6).

Over the years this numerical record is built up until a full 'profile' is completed at the end of year 5. (Figure 12.7) When a P.E. report is written there is often no copy kept by the P.E. department. It is unlikely that teachers will remember exactly what was said previously when the next set of reports are due. This computerised system would allow the teacher to consult the previous figures and knowing that a number 1 stands for excellent down to 5 for poor and a 6 for no comment it becomes possible to detect trends of improvement or regression or just steady progress.

Once you start to consider the introdution of a computerised form of pupil assessment it brings into question the whole nature of what is being taught, how that work is carried out and the methods used to record and assess the work and progress of pupils. There is no doubt that this form of assessment will make the P.E. teacher think more carefully about every pupil as they progress throughout the school.

| PUPIL PROFILE for : | | | YEAR | | |
JOHN SMITH of 1 HAR	1	2	3	4	5
EFFORT	1	0	0	0	0
PARTICIPATION	1	0	0	0	0
ATTITUDE	1	0	0	0	0
CO-OPERATION WITH OTHERS	3	0	0	0	0
LEVEL OF FITNESS	2	0	0	0	0
GYMNASTICS	2	0	0	0	0
SWIMMING	3	0	0	0	0
HOCKEY	2	0	0	0	0

Figure 12.6
The beginning of the pupil profile showing the numerical values of the Year 1 report.

| PUPIL PROFILE for : | | | YEAR | | |
JOHN SMITH of 1 HAR	1	2	3	4	5
EFFORT	1	2	3	2	1
PARTICIPATION	1	3	4	3	2
ATTITUDE	1	3	5	3	2
CO-OPERATION WITH OTHERS	3	4	4	4	3
LEVEL OF FITNESS	2	2	2	3	2
GYMNASTICS	2	3	2	2	2
SWIMMING	3	3	2	2	1
HOCKEY	2	2	3	4	3

Figure 12.7
By the end of Year 5 the pupil profile will be complete.

Reports and Pupil Profiles

Glossary

ACCESS
To obtain data from the computer or from a storage medium like a disc.

ALPHA
Characters which are alphabetic, see also alphanumeric.

ALPHANUMERIC
Characters which are either alphabetic or numeric.

AUDIO CASSETTE
Magnetic tape cassette used for storing data.

BACKUP
A second copy of data for security purposes.

BAR CODE
A sequence of thin and thick lines, as appears on a most food items, which when read by a special device can provide information to a computer.

BAR CODE READER
A device for reading bar codes and transmitting the data to a computer.

BASIC
(Beginner's All-purpose Symbolic Instruction Code) A simple language used in the writing of computer programs.

BOOT
For some older computers it is a term meaning 'to start up' the computer by entering a few items of instructions. In newer models it is now used as a means of loading/starting a computer program from a disc. On the BBC machine this is done by pressing the SHIFT and BREAK keys at the same time.

BREAK
A key on the computer which can interupt a program and stop it working. A key to be used with extreme caution except when starting a program – see BOOT.

BT GOLD
British Telecom Gold, an electronic mail service.

BUGS
Programming errors.

CASSETTE
See audio cassette.

CATALOGUE
A list of contents on a disc.

CEEFAX
The BBC version of Teletext.

CENTRAL PROCESSING UNIT
The main part of the computer where all the processing occurs.

CHARACTER
A symbol used by the computer to represent data.

CHIPS
Solid state electronic components which help to make up the computer.

COMPUTER
An electronic machine whose input and output are determined by the way the device is programmed.

CURSOR
Usually a line on the computer monitor which shows where the next character will be printed.

DAISY WHEEL PRINTER
A printer whose characters are located on the spokes of a rotating ring.

DATA
Coded information which the computer can use, read or produce.

DATABASE
Data which is organised and structured according to the needs of the user. The data can be processed in various ways.

DEBUG
The removal of program errors.

DIGITAL
Being of numerical value

DIP SWITCHES
Small switches in a printer which select various options of operation.

DISC
Magnetised material used for storing computer data.

DISC DRIVE
A device for reading data from or writing data to a rotating disc.

DISK
An alternate way of spelling DISC

DISKETTE
Another word for DISK or DISC

DOCUMENTATION
The instructions which should accompany all software.

DOT MATRIX PRINTER
A printer whose characters are formed by printing a

Glossary

pattern of dots.

DUMP
To transfer data usually from the computer memory to a printer.

ECONET
A number of computers interconnected and linked to one main disc drive. Often used in school computer rooms.

ELECTRONIC MAIL
A means of sending messages from one computer user to another via the telephone.

ERROR
A message produced by the computer which appears on the screen when something goes wrong with a program!

FIELD
One section of a record which holds a single item of data.

FILE
An organised collection of records, just like a filing cabinet.

FLOPPY DISC
See DISC.

FORMATTING
A means of organising the tracks and sectors on a new disc before it can be used.

FRICTION FEED
A means of feeding single sheets through a printer. See also TRACTOR FEED.

FUNCTION KEY
A key on the computer which has been programmed to perform a particular task. (The red keys on a BBC computer are all 'function keys').

GENERATE
To produce some item.

GRAPHIC
Diagrams, shapes or pictures produced by computer programs.

HARD COPY
Computer produced material printed out on paper via a computer printer.

HARD DISC
Used for storing computer data but not normally associated with microcomputers which usually use a 'floppy disc'.

HARDWARE
The equipment, such as the computer, disc drive, printer, etc.

ICON
An image or symbol representing a file or an item. The file is then accessed by pressing a button on a mouse which has moved a pointer over the required icon.

INFORMATION RETRIEVAL
Obtaining specific information from stored data in a database.

INPUT
Putting data into the computer as opposed to 'output'.

JOYSTICK
A device attached to the computer which can be used to move objects on the screen; most commonly used for computer games.

JUSTIFICATION
A means of adding spaces so that certain things line up, like the lining up of the right hand margin of a piece of text so that it appears straight.

K
Stands for 'Kilo' and is a unit of memory for computers. Although it stands for one thousand every 1K does in fact hold 1024 characters of data.

KEYBOARD
The keys on a computer which are usually arranged in the QWERTY typewriter pattern.

LIGHT PEN
A pen like device which can be used to indicate positions on the screen or read off data from bar codes. It is connected directly to the computer.

LOAD
To enter data or a program into the computer.

MACHINE
The computer is often described as a 'machine' since it can perform a wide variety of tasks.

MACHINE CODE
This is a binary set of instructions which can be executed by the computer.

MAINFRAME
A very large computer with a high storage capacity.

MEMORY
The storage capability of a computer.

MENU
A system of presenting a range of options to the user of a program.

MICROCOMPUTER
A computer which uses a microprocessor for its central processing unit.

MICROPROCESSOR
A circuit which contains all the elements of its central processing unit.

MINICOMPUTER
A smaller version of a Mainframe Computer.

MODEM
A device enabling communications to and from different computers via the telephone.

MONITOR
Another word for 'visual display unit' (VDU). It could be a special computer monitor or an ordinary television screen.

MOUSE
A wheeled device which when moved around a table can control a cursor on the screen. A button can be pressed by the fingers to access items shown on the

screen, perhaps from icons.

NLQ
Printers described in this way are able to produce a type of print which is 'near letter quality'.

NUMBER CRUNCHING
Rapid calculations of numerical data.

NUMERIC
Representing a number.

ORACLE
The IBA version of teletext.

OUTPUT
Obtaining data from the computer onto the screen, on paper or to storage.

PAGING
A wordprocessor term allowing the user to print their material a page at a time instead of in a continuous fashion.

PERIPHERALS
Other items of computer hardware which perform various additional but essential functions such as printers or disc drives.

PIXEL
In graphics it refers to the smallest element of a picture, which is the size of one dot.

PLOT
To draw lines or diagrams.

PRESTEL
A viewdata system provided by British Telecom.

PRINTER
Transfers signals from a computer to a readable form on paper.

PRINTOUT
The output produced by the printer.

PROCESSING
The type of work carried out by the computer such as storing, manipulating and sorting data as well as calculating and making decisions.

PROGRAM
The American Version of the word 'programme' but now accepted as meaning the set of instructions which the computer will follow.

PROGRAMMER
The person who writes and updates computer programs.

QUERY
A request for information when using a database.

RANDOM ACCESS MEMORY (RAM)
Memory which is used when reading from the computer or when writing to it. A temporary memory.

READ ONLY MEMORY (ROM)
Memory which can only be read from but never written to. Programs such as a word processor might be kept in ROM. A permanent memory.

RECORD
A number of related pieces of data.

REM
A non-active statement in a computer program to REMind the programmer what is happenning.

RUN
An instruction to start a computer program.

SCREEN
The display part of a VDU or television showing the output from a computer.

SOFTWARE
Computer programs with their instructions.

SPREADSHEET
Used for the storing and analysis of financial or numerical data.

TELETEXT
Information transmitted at the same time as television pictures but only available on special television sets.

TRACTOR FEED
A device for feeding continuous paper through a printer by means of pins engaging in the perforated edges.

USER
A person who is using the computer.

USER FRIENDLY
An easy to use computer program which will prompt the inexperienced user with simple instructions.

VDU
Visual Display Unit or screen or monitor.

WORD PROCESSOR
A computer program which will allow a user to write, edit, store, retrieve and print text.

APPENDIX I

COMPUTER PROGRAMS by MIKE SKINSLEY

Much of this book is based upon the programs written by the author for use in his school or for other sports events. Many of the programs have been used for adult competitions, such as the cross country race analysis programs.

At the time of writing this book the following programs were available for use with the BBC Micro.

1. Cross Country Race Analysis) Three
2. Cross Country Race Analysis) different
3. Cross Country Race Analysis) versions.
4. J.C.R. Fitness test.
5. Options in P.E. Analysis.
6. Sports Day Results Analysis.
7. Year File.

CROSS COUNTRY RACE ANALYSIS

Three versions of this program are available to analyse cross country race results depending on the type of event being organised. In all three programs the user determines the number of counting runners for the Team competition.

CROSS COUNTRY PROGRAM 1

This computer program is designed to analyse a school inter Tutor Group and Inter House cross country race. It will produce a printed list of the Individual Result, the Inter Tutor Group Result, the Inter House Result and a Race Summary Sheet. Details of the positions will be automatically saved on disc and can be retrieved later. A Recording Sheet can be printed out containing all the pupils names on which only the finishing positions need to be written at the end of the race.

CROSS COUNTRY PROGRAM 2

This version of the Cross Country Analysis Program can be used for an Inter School, District or even County competition. It can also be used for an Inter House Race when an Inter Tutor Group competition is not being held at the same time.

This version will produce a Recording Sheet for use at the end of the race. It will also print out an Individual Result, the Team Result and a Race Summary Sheet. The race details will automatically be saved and can be recalled later.

CROSS COUNTRY PROGRAM 3

This version of the Cross Country Analysis Program is for an event where named runners are given numbers. All that needs to be entered into the computer at the end of the race are the runners numbers in the order in which they finish the race.

It will print out the Individual Result, the Team Result and a Race Summary Sheet. The race details will automatically be saved and can be recalled later.

THE J.C.R. FITNESS TEST. PROGRAM 4

The J.C.R. test, comprising of a standing vertical jump, maximum chins to the beam and a 100 yard shuttle run, is designed to measure such elements of fitness as strength, speed, agility and endurance. The test uses a minimum amount of equipment and can be completed relatively quickly. Points are awarded according to performance and an overall score can be related to a grade or level of fitness according to age. The grades range from one (high) to six (low). The scores and grades used in this program have been adapted from original work of the J.C.R. Test by Phillips (1947) and Cooper (1963).

The program has been developed so that the computer is used in the gym whilst

Appendix I

testing is carried out. A print out of all the pupils names with spaces for recording the three results can be produced. As soon as a pupil has completed his three tests he can then use the computer to analyse his performance and obtain a print out of his 'Fitness Grade'. It is also possible to use this program without a printer. The teacher can obtain a summary of all the pupil performances and grades.

OPTIONS IN P.E. ANALYSIS. PROGRAM 5

The task of analysing an Options scheme as part of the Physical Education curriculum can be very time consuming. A computer can be used to assist the Physical Education teacher not only to analyse the results but also to print out the findings.

This specially written 'Options' program is designed so that the user can adapt the program to suit their own circumstances within a certain framework. The program allows for options covering two periods of time. This could be two Half Term periods, for two different terms or for two half year periods.

Any number of activities being offered to the pupils can be inserted easily into the program. The program allows for mixed (boys and girls) groups although it can be run for only one sex.

An analysis can be obtained of the numbers of pupils who have chosen each activity. Print outs can be obtained of all those opting for each activity, with their second and third choice alongside in case adjustments need to be made. A list of pupils who have not made their choices can be seen as can a complete list of all the data on which the analysis is based, i.e. pupil name, tutor group, sex, and choices made. Once adjustments have been made then a list of the final pupil choice can be printed and placed on the notice board. The program will also print out lists for the teacher of all pupils taking part in each activity.

SPORTS DAY RESULTS ANALYSIS. PROGRAM 6

This computer program produces up to the minute scores for different Year groups during the course of running a school Sports Day

programme. At any time during Sports Day, at the press of a button all the running scores of all year groups can be printed out and handed immediately to the announcer.

The program will only analyse the scores and does not involve entering details of competitors names of performances. It is a very efficient way of keeping spectators and athletes informed of the scores without putting any pressure on the scorer(s). Two scorers can operate this system during a very large Sports Day programme of events without any difficulty.

The program has been written for a school with four Houses having competitions across each of the five year groups. However, the program can be adapted or used with a different format of school Sports Day event.

Scores gained in each event by each year group can be viewed. This would show which results sheets were still outstanding and provides a check of the scores entered into the computer.

YEAR FILE. PROGRAM 7

All of the above programs are linked to this master YEAR FILE program in which you enter some basic details of each pupil. This data is then saved onto a disc and is accessed by each program so avoiding the need to keep writing out pupil names.

This program can also be used in its own right for printing out Tutor Group lists, House lists, boys or girls lists, or lists of pupils alphabetically.

ENQUIRIES

Details of the cost of these programs, along with information of other programs which Mike Skinsley has since written, can be obtained by sending a SAE to:

The Ling Book Shop,
162 King's Cross Road,
London WC1X 9DH
Telephone: 01-278 5023

APPENDIX II

OTHER PROGRAMS

The author has examined many P.E. related computer programs and other commercial software. The following list contains some of the known software which may be of particular interest and use to the P.E. specialist. The author has had no personal involvement in the writing of any of these programs, some of which may be found to be more suitable than others.

PROGRAMS

'Steps to Fitness'
from Esmonde Publishing Ltd., The Melbourne Centre, Imperial Road, London SW6.

'PWC170 Fitness Test'
Cranley Medical Electronics, The Sandpits, Acacia Road, Birmingham B30 2AH.

'Reaction tests' from the book 'Sport examined' The book, by Paul Beashel and John Taylor is available from the PEA and details of the computer programs are available from Paul Beashel, 13 Suffolk Road, Seven Rings, Ilford (send SAE).

'Quest' (Database program)
AUCBE, Endymion Road, Hatfield, Herts, AL10 8AU.

'Wordwise' or 'Wordwise Plus' (a wordprocessing chip)
Computer Concepts, Maddesden Place, Hemel Hempstead, Herts, HP2 6EX.

'View' (a wordprocessing chip)
Acorn Computers, 645 Newmarket Road, Cambridge, CB5 8PD.

'Mini Office II' (Wordprocessor, Database, Spreadsheet, Graphics, Communications) Database Publications, Europa House, 68 Chester Road, Hazel Grove, Stockport SK7 5NY or some High Street shops such as W.H. Smiths.

'Fleet Street Editor' Mirrorsoft Ltd, Headington Hill Hall, Oxford, OX3 0BW.

'Balance Your Diet'
Netherhall Software, Cambridge University Press, Cambridge.

'Reactions and Blind Spot'
AVP Computing, Chepstow, Gwent.

APPENDIX III

BOOKS and COURSES

BOOKS

'Microcomputing in Sport and Physical Education'
by D.A. Brodie and J.J. Thornhill
Lepus Books. ISBN 0-86019-106-0
(Many P.E. computer programs are listed for
various computers).

'Projects for Programs'
Ladybird Computer Series. ISBN 0-7214-9514-1
(Simple competition program)

COURSES

For details of P.E. based computer courses send
SAE to:
 The Physical Education Association,
 162 King's Cross Road,
 London WC1X 9DH